★ ★

The American Presidents

D1528685

by Marilynn Barr

Contributing Graphic Artists
Jason Barr
Heather Cox

★ ★

This book is for
B Dot, the Bean,
and
"My Kids,"

Jason R, Leon R, Geoff R, Jason Q, Tracy N, Tracy R, Heather C, Heather P, Jamie F, Sal S, Gray J,
Chris S, Nathan C, Angela F, Anthony J, Vaughn G, Brian F, Brian C, Doris J, Chad P, Perry S, Bryant M,
Patrick S, Jennifer M, Dawn S, Brandy C, Kristi L, Ken W, Wesley B, Will R, Wendy F, Rocky K, KP,
Matt C, Kelly J, Kelly L, David B, Jeff S, Joseph McD, Kim A, Danny T, Bruce K, Jamie McC, Brian G,
Leroy M, Stephanie G, Priscilla P, Himmy C, B Cox, Jason C, Tommy S, Crystal T, Amber C, Wayne L,
Heather W, Katie H, Jason A, Josh A, Scott J, Ross A, Sugarbear, Orlando B, Bobby T, Michael S,
Michael H, Troy F, Anne Marie B, KC C, Susan Marie G, Sammy A, Leigh R, Carlson, Shelby S,
Bowen S, Morgan S, and Stephanie B

Entire contents copyright © 2000 by Monday Morning Books, Inc.,
Box 1680, Palo Alto, California 94302
For a complete catalog, write to the address above.

Call our toll-free number: 1-800-255-6049
E-mail us at: MMBooks@aol.com
Visit our Web site:
http://www.mondaymorningbooks.com

Monday Morning is a registered trademark of
Monday Morning Books, Inc.

Permission is hereby granted to reproduce
student materials in this book for non-commercial
individual or classroom use.

ISBN 1-878279-47-5
Printed in the United States of America
9 8 7 6 5 4 3 2 1

OVAL OFFICE
is an exciting, interactive CD-ROM based on
How to Be President of the U.S.A.
For pricing and other information, contact
MERIDIAN CREATIVE GROUP
5178 Station Road
Erie, PA 16510 • (814) 898-2612

Contents

Introduction

History can be fun. Learn interesting facts about the Presidents and their First Ladies. Practice writing, develop research skills, and create arts and crafts projects that relate to favorite hobbies, pastimes, or historical events that occurred during the lives of the American Presidents.

To Trace Patterns

Materials: wax paper, masking tape, ballpoint pen

Tear and tape a sheet of wax paper over the image you want to trace. Trace the image with a ballpoint pen. You will need to clean the wax from the tip of the pen from time to time.

To Make a Transfer Pattern

Materials: newspaper, smock, masking tape, baby oil, cotton ball, ballpoint pen, blank paper or poster board

Cover your work area with newspaper, put on a smock, and roll up your sleeves. Tape a photocopy or wax paper tracing to a sunlit window. Tape a sheet of butcher paper over it. Use a pencil or marker to trace the image. Remove both sheets from the window. Color the back of the butcher paper tracing with a lead pencil. Apply a small amount of baby oil on a cotton ball and wipe over the pencil lead. This will smear and blend the lead particles. Wipe off excess oil. Attach a masking tape border around your transfer. To use the transfer, tape the corners on top of a blank sheet of paper or poster board. Work on a smooth, flat surface. Trace the lines with a ballpoint pen. Lift a corner to check your progress. Store your transfer patterns in separate folders.

Paper Bag Parchment

Materials: brown paper bag, an adult helper, iron, crayons, markers

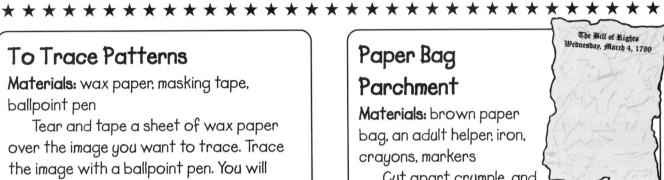

Cut apart, crumple, and tear a page similar to the one shown here from a brown paper bag. Ask an adult to iron the page then discuss the importance of documents like the Declaration of Independence, the Constitution, and the Bill of Rights. Draw pictures or write about what you learned from your discussion on your paper bag parchment.

Growing a Nation Puzzle

Materials: paper, felt, corrugated board, scissors, markers

Make and color a copy of a map of the United States. Glue a piece of felt to the back of the map. Cut the map into puzzle shapes along state boundaries. Glue blue felt to a sheet of corrugated board. Use a marker to draw the outline of the United States on the blue felt board. Then write the name and capital of each state around the edges as a border.

A Presidential Monument

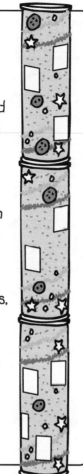

Materials: Collect chip cans and lids, and one plastic coffee can lid to make a Presidential monument.

Glue a coffee can lid to the bottom of one chip can to form a base. Stack and glue the rest of the chip cans to form a tall structure. Use craft supplies such as buttons, ribbon, sequins, stickers, pipe cleaners, and magazine cutouts to decorate the monument. Then copy, color, cut out, and glue portraits and other images in this book to your monument structure.

Presidents Concentration

Materials: 84 index cards, pen or pencil, scissors, glue

Write a fact about each President on separate index cards. Copy, cut out, and glue the President portraits on the remainder of the cards.
To play: Shuffle the cards and place them on a flat surface face down. In turn, each player turns two cards over. If there is a match, the player stacks his cards by his side and continues to play. If there isn't a match, then the next player takes a turn.

Engraved Lockets

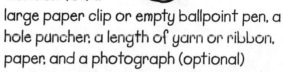

Materials: poster board, pencil, scissors, aluminum foil, a large paper clip or empty ballpoint pen, a hole puncher, a length of yarn or ribbon, paper, and a photograph (optional)

Copy or trace and cut out the locket pattern shown here. Wrap the locket with three layers of foil. Flatten the foil as you wrap. Working on a flat surface, use a large open paper clip or an empty ballpoint pen to draw an engraved design. Draw lightly so you do not tear the foil. Now cut out two oval shapes to fit inside the locket. Ask for a picture that you can cut into an oval or draw a portrait on a paper oval. Write a message on a seond paper oval. Glue both ovals inside the locket. Punch a hole, then thread a length of yarn or ribbon through the top of the locket as shown.

Locket Pattern

★ ★

1 • George Washington
1789-1797

Born: February 22, 1732
Died: December 14, 1799

George Washington never lived in Washington, D.C. Mount Vernon was his home for 45 years. He turned Mount Vernon into a working farm. The dining room at Mount Vernon was designed by George. The walls were painted green and decorated with farm images. The gardens and greenhouse included plant gifts such as larkspur, foxglove, and boxwoods.

Welcome to Mount Vernon

A Shoe Box Diorama

Materials: pencil, paper or poster board, shoe box, construction paper, crayons, markers, scissors, glue

Create a diorama of George Washington's beloved Mount Vernon. Copy or trace the Mount Vernon patterns. Cover and line the shoe box with construction paper. Color, cut out, and glue the patterns inside the shoe box. Copy the sign shown here or design one of your own to welcome viewers.

Farm Friends Trunk

Materials: pencil, four index cards, scissors, shoe box and lid, green construction paper, white crayon

Copy or trace the farm animal stencils onto index cards. Cut out the farm animals to form stencils. Cover the box and lid with green construction paper. Position a stencil on the box, outline it, and fill it in with white crayon. Finish decorating the box with white crayon.

★ ★ ★ ★ ★ ★ ★ ★ ★ ★ ★ ★ ★ ★ ★ ★

Martha Washington recycled her gowns and organized collections of warm clothes for soldiers.

Collect for the Needy

Decorate grocery bags as shown here or create your own design. Collect clothing and other items for the needy. Ask an adult to help you find organizations to accept the collected items.

Don't throw away that shirt, those shoes, sweater... Give it to someone else who can use it! We will be collecting your donations on Saturday. Thank you for your kindness.

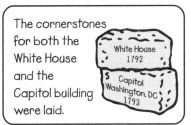

The cornerstones for both the White House and the Capitol building were laid.

White House 1792

Capitol Washington, DC 1793

George Washington was the first President to appear on a postal stamp in 1847.

Mount Vernon

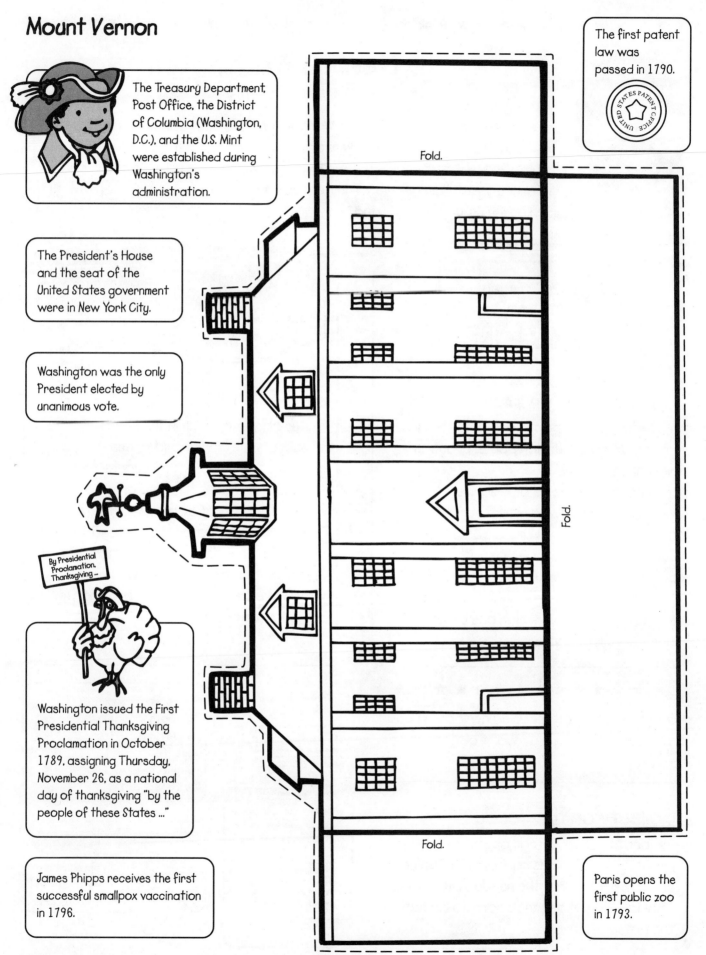

The Treasury Department, Post Office, the District of Columbia (Washington, D.C.), and the U.S. Mint were established during Washington's administration.

The President's House and the seat of the United States government were in New York City.

Washington was the only President elected by unanimous vote.

By Presidential Proclamation, Thanksgiving ...

Washington issued the First Presidential Thanksgiving Proclamation in October 1789, assigning Thursday, November 26, as a national day of thanksgiving "by the people of these States ..."

James Phipps receives the first successful smallpox vaccination in 1796.

The first patent law was passed in 1790.

UNITED STATES PATENT OFFICE

Fold.

Fold.

Fold.

Paris opens the first public zoo in 1793.

The American Presidents ©2000 Monday Morning Books, Inc.

★ ★ ★ ★ ★ ★ ★ ★ ★ ★ ★ ★ ★ ★ ★ ★ ★ ★

Fans decorated with medallion portraits of George Washington were given as souvenirs at the First Inaugural Ball in May 1789.

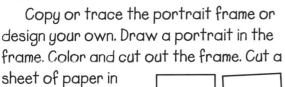

Medallion Fans

Materials: pencil, paper, crayons, markers, scissors, glue, stapler, star stickers, ribbon

Copy or trace the portrait frame or design your own. Draw a portrait in the frame. Color and cut out the frame. Cut a sheet of paper in half lengthwise. 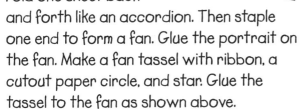 Fold one sheet back and forth like an accordion. Then staple one end to form a fan. Glue the portrait on the fan. Make a fan tassel with ribbon, a cutout paper circle, and star. Glue the tassel to the fan as shown above.

Forks of Tar Rivers, NC, was the first town named for George Washington. The name was changed to Washington in 1775.

Gas lighting of a home accomplished by William Murdock of Scotland in 1792.

★ ★ ★ ★ ★ ★ ★ ★ ★ ★ ★ ★ ★ ★ ★ ★ ★ ★

Washington's favorite occupation was planting and experimenting with new crops. This earned him the affectionate nickname "farmer George."

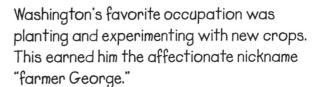

cotton	paper	salt	vinegar	powder	soil	water	light

(table title: What Do Seeds Need to Grow?)

What Do Seeds Need to Grow?

Materials: Styrofoam egg carton, measuring spoons, salt, talcum powder, potting soil, dry beans, spray bottle, paper or poster board, pencil

Fill six egg carton cups as follows:

2 cups with soil and 1 tablespoon salt,
2 cups with soil and 1 tablespoon talcum powder,
2 cups with plain soil

Place two or three beans in each cup. Place the egg carton where it can receive a lot of sun. Use a spray bottle to water each day. Copy the "What Do Seeds Need to Grow?" chart shown above. Record what you discover each day.

George enjoyed raising livestock. In 1785, Spain sent Washington a gift of two jacks and two jennets. He named the surviving jack "Royal Gift" and used it to breed heavy mules.

According to the old style Julian calendar, George Washington's birthday was on February 11, 1732. However, it changed to February 22 when the Gregorian calendar was adopted.

Eli Whitney of the United States invented the cotton gin in 1793.

Mount Vernon Patterns

Henri-Louis Jaquet-Droz and Leschot invented the wristwatch in 1790.

Portrait Frame

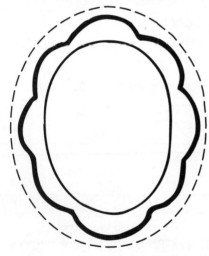

Farm Animal Stencils

 Vermont was admitted as the 14th state March 4, 1791.

 Kentucky was admitted as the 15th state on June 1, 1792.

 Tennessee was admitted as the 16th state on June 1, 1796.

The American Presidents ©2000 Monday Morning Books, Inc.

★ ★

2 • John Adams
1797-1801

As a youngster, John Adams enjoyed flying kites, shooting marbles, and swimming. He joined a reading club in college where members read aloud. He eventually began collecting books for his private library. John Adams also kept a diary. He recorded detailed descriptions of events in his life.

Born: October 19, 1735
Died: July 4, 1826

Make a Diary and Quill Pen

Materials: corrugated board, scissors, gift wrap, crayons, markers, blank paper, hole punch, ribbon, tape, pencil or pen

Cut two 6" x 9" sheets of corrugated board for covers. Fold a 1" margin on the left side of each board. Cover the boards with gift wrap. Decorate the covers. Cut 6" x 9" sheets of paper for diary pages. Copy or trace "Old English" initials onto your diary pages or design your own. Punch two holes along the left side of each page and cover. Lace and tie ribbon through the holes. Now you are ready to write in your diary.

To make a quill pen: Color a corner of a sheet of paper. Roll the paper into a tube as shown. Secure the tube with a piece of tape. Cut a 2" fringe around the end with the colored corner. Hold the tube in your left hand and remove the tape. Using your right hand, carefully pull the colored corner out of the tube. This will form a fringed feather. Insert a pencil or pen in the open end and secure the feather with tape.

Reading Club

Materials: pencil, paper, scissors, glue, construction paper, crayons, markers

Copy or trace the reading club invitation or design your own. Glue the invitation to a sheet of construction paper. Trim around the invitation. Leave a margin as shown. Write the date and time inside and ask each person to bring a book to share.

John Adams was the only President whose son became President.

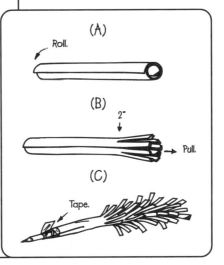

(A) Roll.

(B) 2" Pull.

(C) Tape.

John Adams originally wrote these words to his wife. They are now inscribed on the mantle of the State dining room in the White House.

"... May none but honest and wise men ever rule under this roof."

Reading Club Invitation

The Library of Congress was established on April 24, 1800.

John Adams wrote the constitution for the state of Massachusetts.

Old English Initials

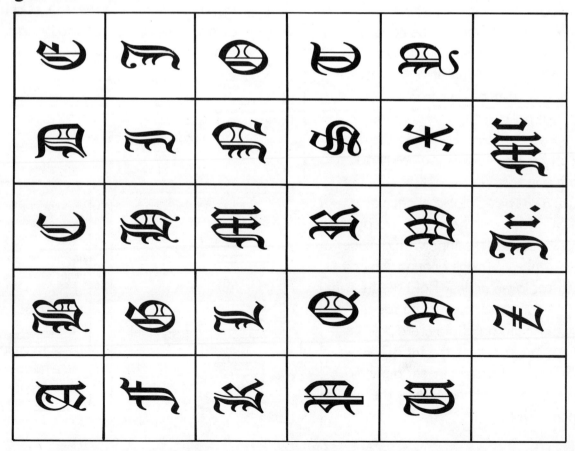

The American Presidents ©2000 Monday Morning Books, Inc.

★ ★ ★ ★ ★ ★ ★ ★ ★ ★ ★ ★ ★ ★ ★ ★

John Adams' favorite pastime was tramping through the woods. He enjoyed hunting deer, squirrels, and other wildlife.

Wildlife Watcher's Journal

Materials: poster board, scissors, blank paper, permanent marker, magazines, old greeting cards, hole punch, twine

Cut two 5" x 7" poster board covers. Make several copies of the journal page or cut blank paper to fit inside your journal. Decorate the cover with wildlife drawings, cutouts from magazines, or old greeting cards. Punch two holes along the left side of each page and cover. Lace and tie two or three lengths of twine through the holes. Record how local wildlife responds to the weather, people, and noise. Record when they sleep, what and how they eat.

★ ★ ★ ★ ★ ★ ★ ★ ★ ★ ★ ★ ★ ★ ★ ★

In 1777, John Adams recommended that Congress establish the design of the United States flag. The design included 13 red and white stripes and 13 stars, one for each of the original 13 colonies, on a blue background.

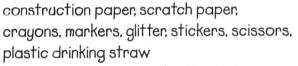

Create a Flag

Materials: pencil, poster board, construction paper, scratch paper, crayons, markers, glitter, stickers, scissors, plastic drinking straw

Imagine you were asked to design a flag for your country. Copy or trace the flag pattern onto poster board or construction paper. Use a combination of 13 stars and stripes or create a new design. Color and decorate your flag with crayons, markers, glitter, stickers, or paper scraps. Cut out the flag and glue it to a plastic straw. Display your flag in a potted plant, a window, or other visible location.

John Adams was the first President to live in the White House in Washington, D.C. It was formerly known as the executive mansion.

The United States' first war ships, also called frigates, were named *Constellation*, *United States*, and *Constitution*. The *Constitution* was also known as "Old Ironsides."

Abigail Adams used the White House's great audience room as a laundry facility while the mansion was being completed.

Flag

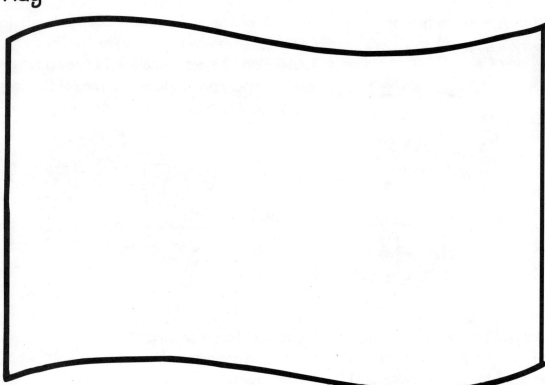

Alessandro Volta invented the electric battery in 1800.

The submarine was invented by Robert Fulton in 1800.

Journal Page

The American Presidents ©2000 Monday Morning Books, Inc.

★★★★★★★★★★★★★★★★★★★★★★★★★★★★★★★★★★★★★★★

3 • Thomas Jefferson
1801-1809

Born: April 13, 1743
Died: July 4, 1826

Thomas Jefferson enjoyed the woods, observing nature, books, and architecture. He kept detailed records of plant life and weather conditions at Monticello. In 1769, he began building historical Monticello. The 21-room mansion featured unusual architectural designs. It had a two-faced clock, which showed the time both indoors and outdoors. It also had a retractable wall bed and an indoor-outdoor weather vane. Thomas Jefferson had two book collections. The first was lost in a fire. The second grew to 6,500 volumes.

A Monticello Weather Calendar

Materials: pencil, poster board, crayons, markers, scissors, hole punch, three brass fasteners

Copy the weather calendar patterns onto poster board. Color and cut out the patterns. Punch a hole at each gray dot on the building. Cut out each gray rectangle and the center of the dome. Program the date wheels as directed. Then punch a hole in the center of each wheel. Attach each wheel to the back of the building with a brass fastener. Turn the wheels to show the month, date, and weather each day. Make more weather wheels to reflect other weather conditions.

President Jefferson introduced handshaking at the White House in 1801. This gesture replaced the more formal bow.

Ohio was admitted as the 17th state on March 1, 1803.

Book Collector Book Plates

Materials: pencil, paper, crayons, markers, scissors, pen, tape

Copy or trace the book plates or design your own. Color and cut out the book plates. Write your name on each plate. Tape a book plate on the inside of each book in your collection.

Jefferson Collection Math

Thomas Jefferson lived to be 83 years old. The United States purchased his book collection for $23,950. The books were transported to Washington, D.C., in 11 wagons. Imagine if you had 6,500 books. Would they fit in your bedroom? How many books would you have to buy each year, month, week, to have 6,500? How much would you spend if each book cost $8.95? How much did the United States pay for each book in Jefferson's collection? How many books fit in each wagon? Ask a friend or family member to help you do the math.

Monticello Weather Calendar

Ultraviolet rays were discovered in 1802 by Johann Wilhelm Ritter.

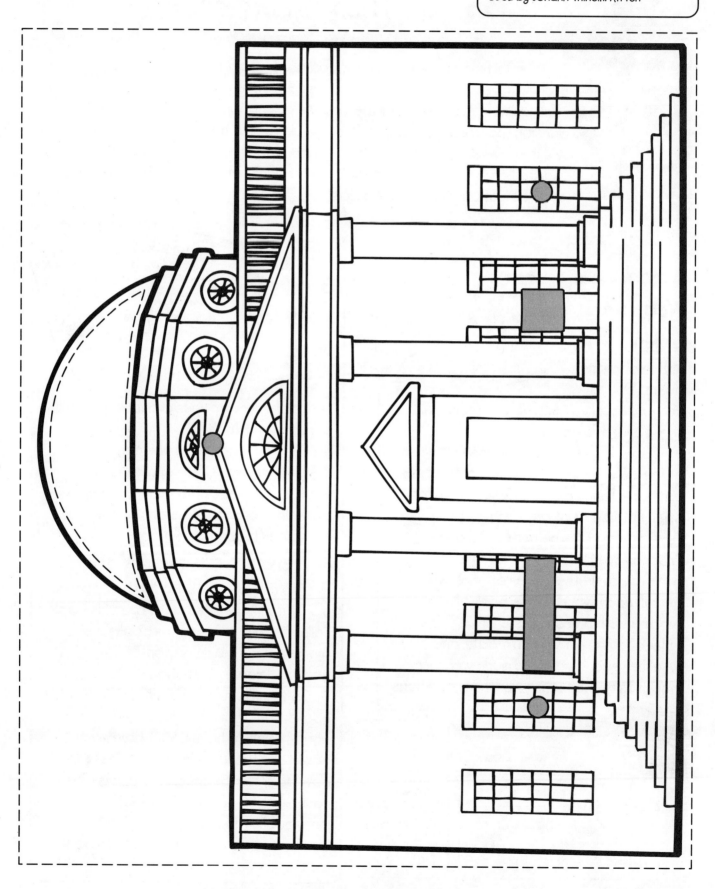

The American Presidents ©2000 Monday Morning Books, Inc.

Monticello Weather Calendar Wheels

Make two copies of the date wheel.
Program one wheel with numbers 1-16.
Program the second wheel with
numbers 17-31.

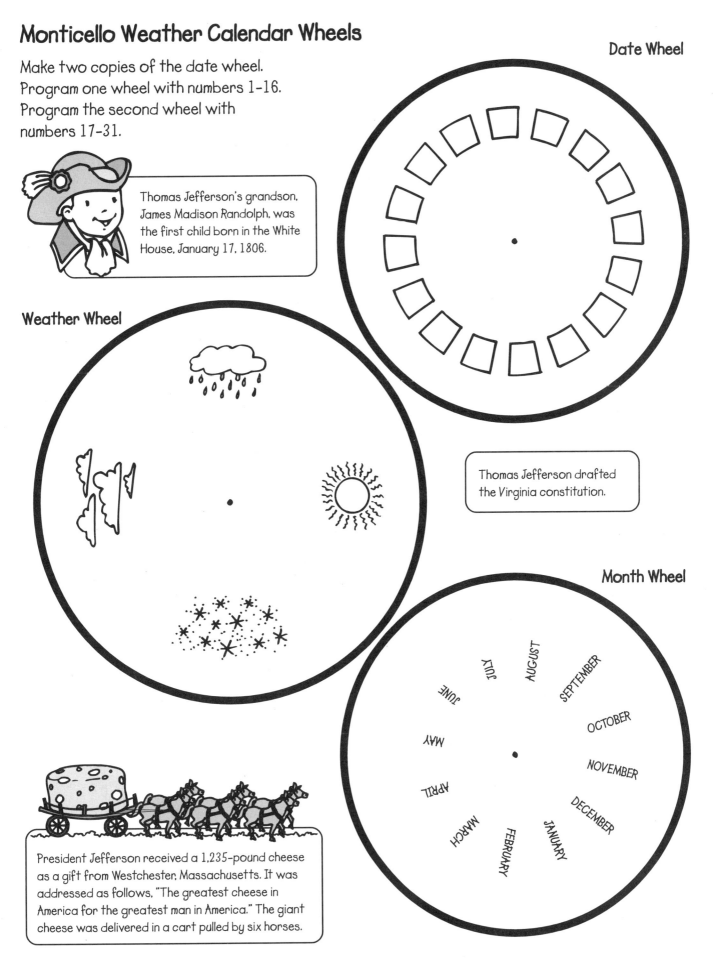

Thomas Jefferson's grandson,
James Madison Randolph, was
the first child born in the White
House, January 17, 1806.

Date Wheel

Weather Wheel

Thomas Jefferson drafted
the Virginia constitution.

Month Wheel

JULY
AUGUST
SEPTEMBER
OCTOBER
NOVEMBER
DECEMBER
JANUARY
FEBRUARY
MARCH
APRIL
MAY
JUNE

President Jefferson received a 1,235-pound cheese
as a gift from Westchester, Massachusetts. It was
addressed as follows, "The greatest cheese in
America for the greatest man in America." The giant
cheese was delivered in a cart pulled by six horses.

Book Plates

The American Presidents ©2000 Monday Morning Books, Inc.

President Jefferson sent his secretary, Meriwether Lewis, and a frontiersman, William Clark, on a journey across the nation. On May 14, 1804, Lewis and Clark left St. Louis, Missouri. They returned on September 23, 1806, 28 months later.

On April 30, 1803, the United States agreed to pay France $11,250,000 for the Louisiana Purchase territory. This transaction nearly doubled the size of the United States. The territory would later become all or part of Arkansas, Colorado, Iowa, Kansas, Louisiana, Minnesota, Missouri, Montana, Nebraska, North and South Dakota, Oklahoma, and Wyoming.

On August 7, 1807, Robert Fulton's steamboat, *Clermont*, made a trip on the Hudson River.

Respectfully Yours, Lewis and Clark

Materials: stationery, envelopes, scissors, glue, book about Lewis and Clark, pencil, pen, crayons, markers

Make a copy of the expedition map. Glue it to the first page of your letter. Read about Lewis and Clark's adventure. Imagine you were invited to travel with them on their historical 28-month journey. Write a letter to your parents about your trip. Answer the following questions to get your letter started. What did you eat? Where did you get your food? How did you travel? Where did you sleep? How many miles did you travel each day? What was the weather like? Did you encounter danger? Did you make any friends?

Lewis & Clark Expedition Map

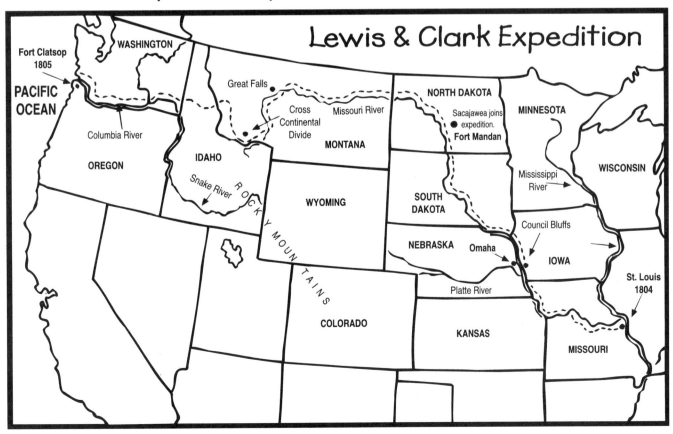

4 • James Madison
1809-1817

Born: March 16, 1751
Died: June 28, 1836

Montpelier was James Madison's home for most of his life. During his term as President, James and Dolley Madison were forced to move from the White House. Dolley Madison rescued the National Seal, the original draft of the Constitution, the Declaration of Independence, and a full-length portrait of George Washington. The British burned down the White House in August of 1814.

Montpelier Bean Mosaic

Materials: construction paper, pencil, scissors, glue, poster or card board, beans, crayons or markers

Make a copy or trace the Montpelier pattern onto a sheet of construction paper. Cut out and glue Montpelier to a sheet of poster or card board. Use a variety of beans to create a bean mosaic of James Madison's home. Decorate the rest of Montpelier with crayons or markers.

A Heroine's Scrapbook

Materials: poster board, scissors, construction paper, doilies, crayons, markers, glue, hole punch, ribbon or yarn

Cut a 11" x 22" sheet from poster board. Divide the poster board into thirds to form a portfolio with 3 panels as shown above. Decorate the outside of the portfolio with construction paper, doilies, crayons, and markers. Cut out and glue construction paper to each panel. Copy or trace, color, and cut out the scrapbook patterns. Glue the patterns inside the scrapbook. Punch a hole in the center front panel as shown. Cut a length of ribbon or yarn long enough to wrap around the closed scrapbook. Lace it through the hole. To close the scrapbook portfolio, fold the right then the left panel. Wrap and tie the ribbon in a bow.

James Madison enjoyed horseback riding, walking, and observing nature.

Francis Scott Key wrote the "Star Spangled Banner" on September 13, 1814.

The American Presidents ©2000 Monday Morning Books, Inc.

Montpelier

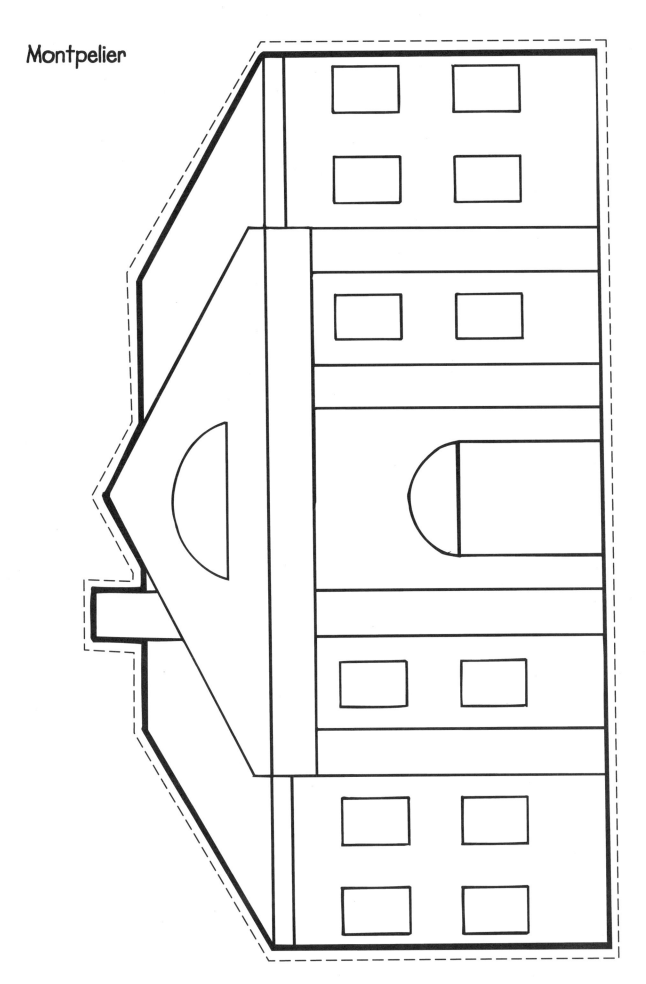

Dolley Madison's choice of clothing and jewelry set fashion trends in America. She was known for wearing elaborate jeweled and feathered turbans.

A Feathered Headdress

Materials: poster board, pencil, construction paper, crayons, markers, glitter, scissors, glue, stapler

Cut a 2" x 22" strip from poster board. Wrap it around your head and staple the ends together to form a headband. Copy or trace several construction paper feathers. Cut out the feathers and staple or glue them around the headband. Cut out construction paper jewel shapes and glue them to your headband. Add sparkle to your headband with glitter.

Washington Monument
July 4, 1815

The cornerstone of the first monument to George Washington was laid at Baltimore, Maryland, on July 4, 1815.

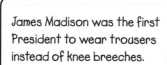

Finally! Long pants!

James Madison was the first President to wear trousers instead of knee breeches.

Parrots became very popular when Dolley Madison chose a macaw as a pet.

A Patriotic Parrot

Materials: pencil, paper, poster board, red, white, and blue construction paper, crayons, markers, scissors, glue (optional: paper towel roll and plastic coffee can lid)

Trace or copy the parrot pattern. Color and glue the pattern to a sheet of poster board. Cut out red, white, and blue construction paper feathers. Starting at the neck, glue the feathers to the parrot. Overlap each layer. Decorate the border. **To make a free-standing display:** Cut out the parrot before you glue the feathers. Wrap and glue a sheet of construction paper or gift wrap around a paper towel tube. Apply a line of glue to the back of the parrot and attach it to the tube. Place the tube, parrot facedown, on a flat surface to dry. When it is dry, glue the tube to a plastic coffee can lid.

Louisiana was admitted as the 18th state on April 30, 1812.

Indiana was admitted as the 19th state on December 11, 1816.

The American Presidents ©2000 Monday Morning Books, Inc.

Scrapbook Patterns

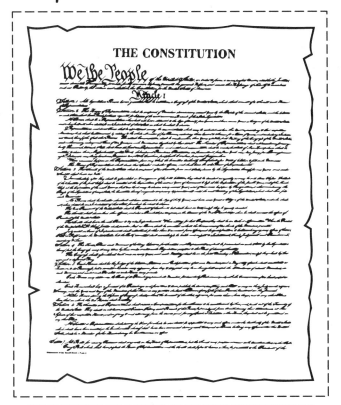

The Constitution

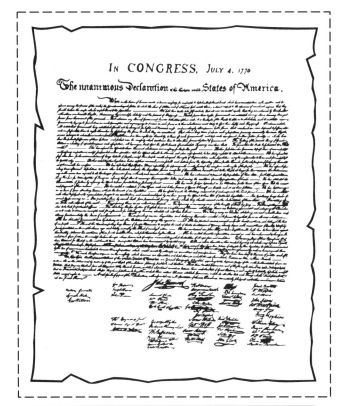

The Declaration of Independence

Portrait of George Washington

The Great Seal
of the United States

Parrot

Headdress Feathers

 The American Presidents ©2000 Monday Morning Books, Inc.

★ ★

5 • James Monroe
1817-1825

James Monroe's administration was described as the "Era of Good Feelings." In 1906, a secret compartment was discovered in James Monroe's desk. It contained letters from Thomas Jefferson and Lafayette. One of Jefferson's letters read as follows: "How little do my countrymen know what precious blessings they are in possession of, and which no other people on earth enjoy."

Born: April 28, 1758
Died: July 4, 1831

Good Feelings in America

Materials: pencil, construction paper, crayons, markers, glue, scissors, old magazines, stamps

Copy or trace and cut out construction paper postcards and pencil toppers. Decorate with crayons, markers, and magazine cutouts that reflect the "good feelings" in America today.

Pencil Toppers: Cut slits where indicated. Slide a pencil through the slits as shown.

Postcards: Write a message to a pen pal, classmate, or family member. Address, attach a stamp, and mail your postcard.

What's in James Monroe's Desk?

"How little do my countrymen know what precious blessings they are in possession of, and which no other people on earth enjoy."
Thomas Jefferson

Materials:
pencil, paper, construction paper, poster board, crayons, markers, scissors, glue, tape, Post-it Note

Cut and fold a sheet of poster board to form a 6" x 8" card. Copy or trace the desk patterns onto construction paper. Color, cut out, and glue the desk pattern to the front of the card. Color, cut it out, and attach the drop leaf with a tape hinge. Write a message on a Post-it Note and place it under the drop leaf. Read about James Monroe. On the inside of the card, write about or draw objects that might have been found in Monroe's desk.

James Monroe was the first President to ride in a steamboat on May 11, 1819.

On August 15, 1824, Upper Guinea, West Africa, changed its name to Liberia. It named its capital city Monrovia in honor of President Monroe.

Monrovia

James Monroe presented the *Monroe Doctrine* to Congress on December 2, 1823. This document stated that the Americas were not available and would not become available for settlement by any European nations.

Good Feelings Postcard and Pencil Toppers

Place Stamp Here

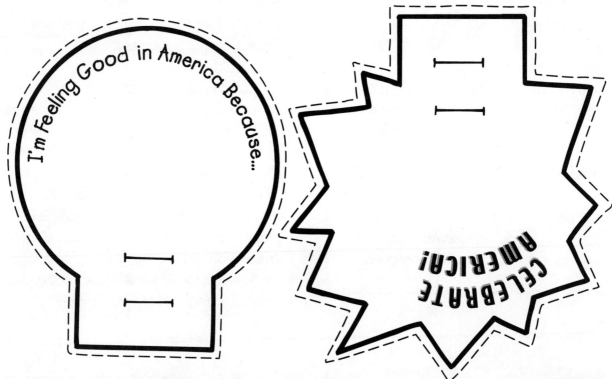

I'm Feeling Good in America Because...

CELEBRATE AMERICA!

Mississippi was admitted as the 20th state on December 10, 1817.

Illinois was admitted as the 21st state on December 3, 1818.

Alabama was admitted as the 22nd state on December 14, 1819.

Maine was admitted as the 23rd state on March 15, 1820.

Missouri was admitted as the 24th state on August 10, 1821.

The American Presidents ©2000 Monday Morning Books, Inc.

James Monroe's Desk Patterns

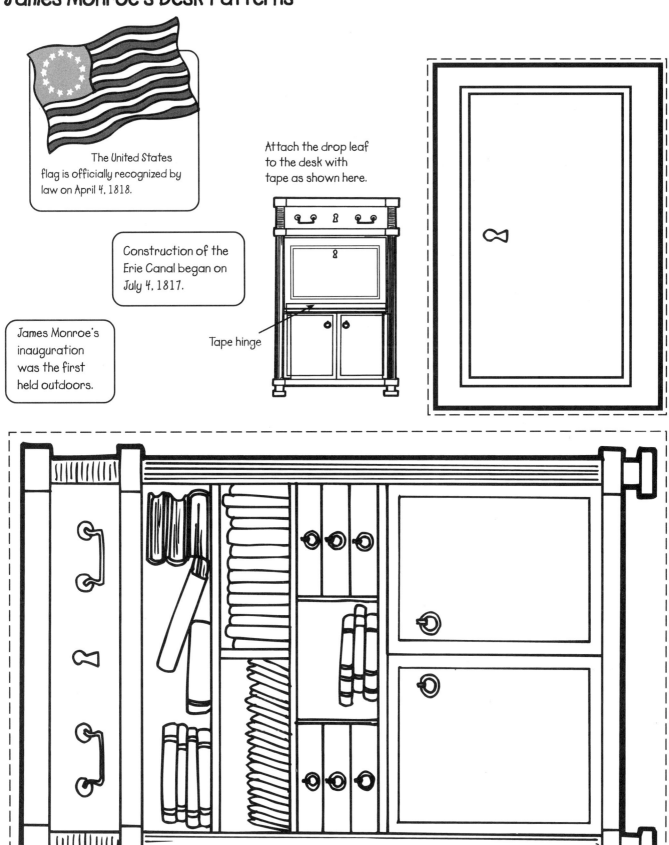

The United States flag is officially recognized by law on April 4, 1818.

Attach the drop leaf to the desk with tape as shown here.

Construction of the Erie Canal began on July 4, 1817.

Tape hinge

James Monroe's inauguration was the first held outdoors.

Glue the desk pattern to a sheet of construction paper or cardbaord.

★ ★

6 • John Quincy Adams
1825-1829

Born: July 11, 1767
Died: February 23, 1848

John Quincy Adams enjoyed playing billiards, reading, and observing nature. He showed very little interest in fashion and was known for wearing the same hat for ten years. Four generations of the Adams family called Franklin Street in Quincy, Massachusetts, home. Two family homes and the United First Parish church are part of the Adams National Historic Site in Quincy.

An Adams Family Village

Materials: pencil, plain and construction paper, crayons, markers, scissors, tape or glue, shoe box lid, paper clips

Copy, color, and cut out an Adams Family Village onto construction paper. Line the inside of a shoe box lid with green construction paper. Tape or glue the fences and bushes along the outside edges of the box lid. Unfold and tape a small paper clip to the back of each pattern for support. Arrange the buildings and trees inside the box lid.

The Erie Canal opened in 1825.

At the age of 15, John Quincy Adams traveled alone for six months to Sweden, Denmark, Germany, and France.

If a Hat Could Talk

I remember when President Adams ...

Materials: pencil, paper, crayons, markers, scissors, glue, small grocery bag, an audience

Choose one of the events listed below to read about. Imagine you were John Quincy Adams' hat, then write about the event. Make a talking hat puppet to narrate your story. Trace or copy the tricorn hat. Color, cut out, and glue it to the bottom of a small grocery bag as shown here. Ask friends or family to listen to a talking hat tell a story about John Quincy Adams.

1755–John Adams teaches school at Worcester, Massachusetts.
1776–John Quincy Adams' father, John Adams, signs the Declaration of Independence.
1797–The frigate, *Constitution*, also known as "Old Ironsides," is launched.
1797–John Quincy Adams' father becomes President.
1825–John Quincy Adams becomes President.
1829–John Quincy Adams retires to his farm.
1846–Neptune is discovered by Johann Gottfield Galle and Heinrich Ludwig d'Arrest.

An Adams Family Village

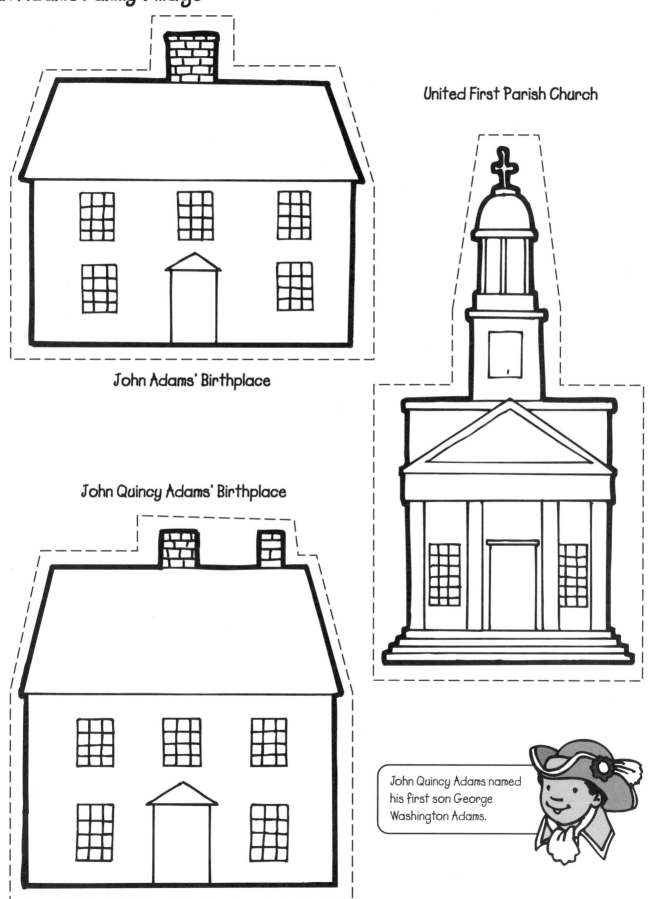

John Adams' Birthplace

United First Parish Church

John Quincy Adams' Birthplace

John Quincy Adams named his first son George Washington Adams.

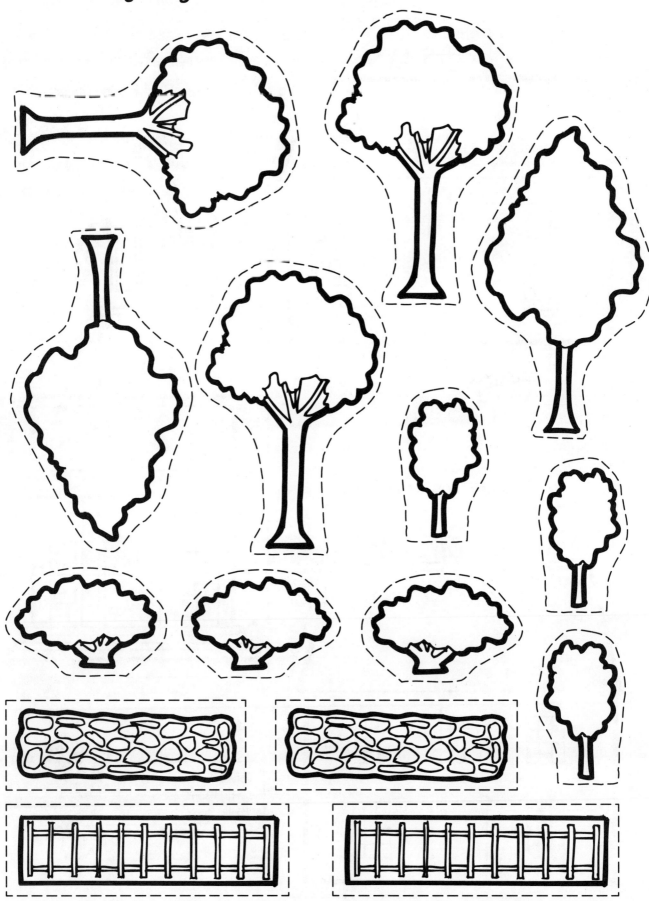

The American Presidents ©2000 Monday Morning Books, Inc.

Tricorn Hat

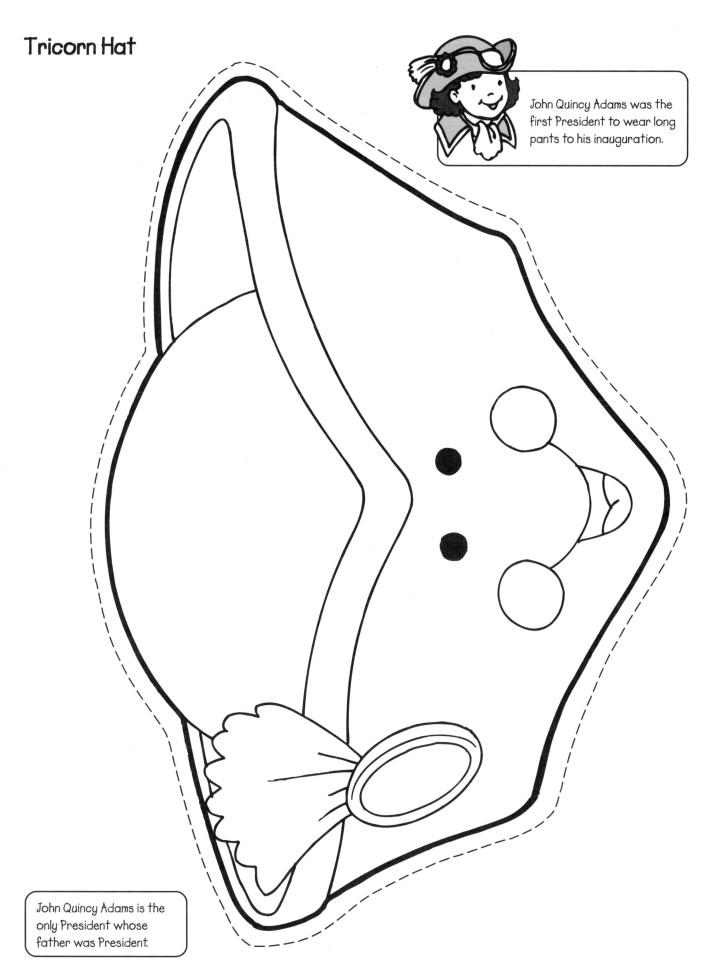

John Quincy Adams was the first President to wear long pants to his inauguration.

John Quincy Adams is the only President whose father was President.

★ ★

7 • Andrew Jackson
1829-1837

Born: March 15, 1767
Died: June 8, 1845

Andrew Jackson was the first President born in a log cabin. Young Andrew read the published Declaration of Independence aloud to the residents of his hometown. He enjoyed raising and racing horses. President Jackson had a large collection of pipes from all over the world. His favorite was a corncob pipe. He also wore a miniature ivory portrait of his late wife, Rachel.

A Pretzel Log Cabin

Materials: cardboard, pretzel sticks, wax paper, tape, peanut butter, plastic knife, adult helper

Ask an adult to help you design your log cabin. Determine how tall and wide it will be. Wrap wax paper around a sheet of sturdy cardboard for a foundation and secure with tape. Use peanut butter as mortar to build your log cabin. Break pretzels in half to fit on either side of doors. Place your finished cabin in the refrigerator to stiffen the peanut butter until you are ready to display it.

Miniature Portraits

Materials: pencil, paper, scissors, glue, poster board, crayons, markers, small photograph, tape, large safety pin

Ask a parent for a small photograph. Copy and glue a portrait frame to a sheet of poster board. When it is dry, color and cut out the frame. Trim and glue a photograph to the frame. Tape a large safety pin to the back.

Bubble Pipe Collage

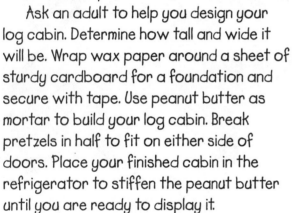

Materials: pencil, construction paper, wallpaper, gift wrap, sandpaper, fabric or leather scraps, grocery bag, poster board, crayons, markers, scissors, glue, aluminum foil, hole punch, yarn

Decide what size you will make your collage and draw a rough sketch. Copy or trace and cut out the pipes from any of the materials listed. Cut two sheets of poster board to make a frame. One should be 4" smaller than the other. Color or decorate a 2" border around the large sheet. Glue the sheets together to form a frame. Glue the pipe or pipes in place. Color bright bubbles on a sheet of aluminum foil. Cut out and glue the bubbles to your collage. When the glue has dried, punch two holes at the top of your picture. Lace and tie a length of yarn through each hole to hang your work.

The American Presidents ©2000 Monday Morning Books, Inc.

Andrew Jackson's actual place of birth is not known. It may have been Lancaster County, South Carolina, or what is now Union County, North Carolina. Each year since 1979, the winner of a high school football game between the two counties settles the question.

Football Classic Checkers

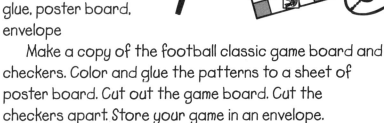

Materials: crayons, markers, scissors, glue, poster board, envelope

Make a copy of the football classic game board and checkers. Color and glue the patterns to a sheet of poster board. Cut out the game board. Cut the checkers apart. Store your game in an envelope.

Bubble Pipe Patterns

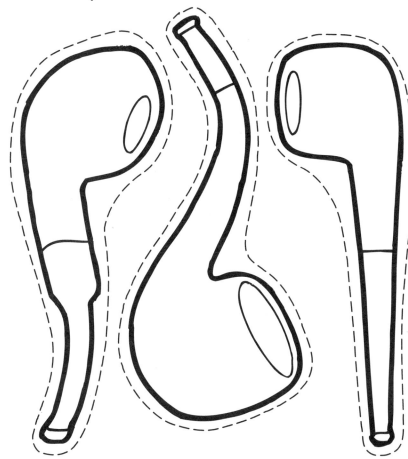

Miniature Frame

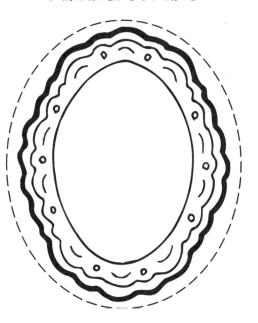

The historic battle at the Alamo took place on March 6, 1836.

Arkansas was admitted as the 25th state on June 15, 1836.

Michigan was admitted as the 26th state on January 26, 1837.

Texas declared independence from Mexico on March 1, 1836.

Football Classic Game Board and Checkers

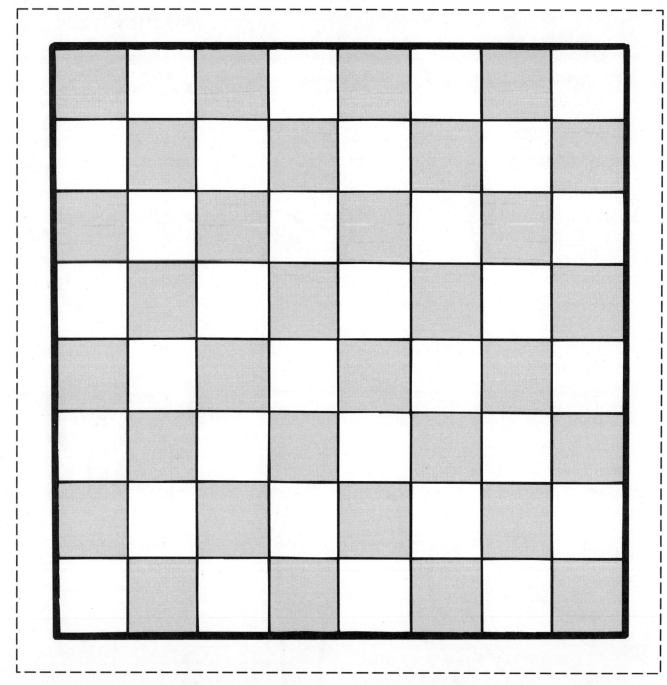

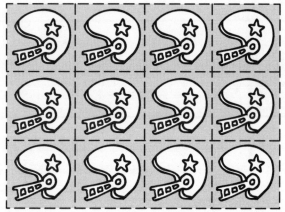
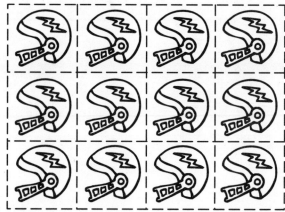

The American Presidents ©2000 Monday Morning Books, Inc.

★ ★

8 • Martin Van Buren
1837-1841

Born: December 5, 1782
Died: July 24, 1862

Martin Van Buren was the first President born as a United States citizen. He enjoyed listening to political conversations as a youngster. Martin Van Buren also enjoyed the theater and fishing. His political skills and actions earned him the nickname of "the Little Magician." In retirement, he enjoyed working his potato crops in Kinderhook, New York.

A Poster for the "Little Magician"

The Little Magician

Materials: poster board, crayons, markers, stickers, paper scraps

Read about Martin Van Buren and why he earned the nickname "Little Magician." Then use crayons, markers, stickers, and paper scraps to design a poster for "The Little Magician." Write a descriptive paragraph on the poster.

Fishy Potato Paintings

Materials:
adult helper, pencil, paper, newspaper, potatoes, paring knife, crayons, markers, margarine tub lids, tempera paint, construction paper

Cover your work surface with newspaper. Ask an adult to help you copy and carve a fish stencil shape on a potato half. Pour paint into a margarine tub lid. Decorate a sheet of construction paper with crayon or marker waves. Dip your potato stencil in paint and stamp fish over the waves.

On January 8, 1838, Alfred Vail dispatched a telegraph message using dots and dashes.

In 1840, OK became an English language expression. It was the abbreviation for Martin Van Buren's nickname, "Old Kinderhook." The Democrats used it as a political slogan. It meant, and still means, all is correct.

Martin Van Buren, William Henry Harrison, and John Tyler all served as President in 1841.

Charles Goodyear obtained a patent for rubber on June 17, 1837.

Fish Stencils

Morse Code Symbols

A ●▬	B ▬●●●	C ▬●▬●	D ▬●●	E ●
F ●●▬●	G ▬▬●	H ●●●●	I ●●	J ●▬▬▬
K ▬●▬	L ●▬●●	M ▬▬	N ▬●	O ▬▬▬
P ●▬▬●	Q ▬▬●▬	R ●▬●	S ●●●	T ▬
U ●●▬	V ●●●▬	W ●▬▬	X ▬●●▬	Y ▬●▬▬
Z ▬▬●●	1 ●▬▬▬▬	2 ●●▬▬▬	3 ●●●▬▬	4 ●●●●▬
5 ●●●●●	6 ▬●●●●	7 ▬▬●●●	8 ▬▬▬●●	9 ▬▬▬▬●
0 ▬▬▬▬▬	Period ●▬●▬●▬	Comma ▬▬●●▬▬	Interrogation ●●▬▬●●	Colon ▬▬▬●●●
Semicolon ▬●▬●▬●	Quotation Marks ●▬●●▬●	SOS ●●●▬▬▬●●●	Start ▬●▬	Wait ●▬●●●
	End of Message ●▬●▬●	Understand ●●▬	Error ●●●●●●●●	

The American Presidents ©2000 Monday Morning Books, Inc.

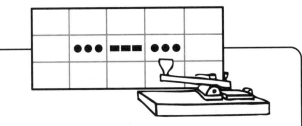

Morse Code Messages

Materials: paper, pencil, index cards, empty coffee cans

Ask a friend to join you in writing Morse code messages. Make 2 copies of the Morse Code Symbols, one for you and one for your friend. Write your name or a simple message like "Hello" on one side of an index card. Write the matching Morse code word or words on the other side. Practice tapping the Morse code alphabet on the bottom of empty coffee can. A dot is a short tap. A dash is a tap with a slight pause. Listen as you tap to recognize the dot and dash pattern.

Louis Braille developed a 43-symbol writing system for the blind in 1837. Raised dot combinations that represent letters and numerals are read by touch.

Braille Alphabet Chart

	a	b	c	
d	e	f	g	h
i	j	k	l	m
n	o	p	q	r
s	t	u	v	w
	x	y	z	

In 1836, John Deere invented the steel plough.

A Mini Potato Patch

Materials: newspaper, pencil, paper, scissors, glue, craft stick, flower pot, potting soil, water, potatoes, paring knife, adult helper, spray bottle

Cover your work area with newspaper. Copy or trace a poster board Potato Patch label. Glue the label to a craft stick. Fill a flower pot $2/3$ full with potting soil. Pour $1/2$ cup water in the soil. Ask an adult to help you cut a potato into sections (each section must have at least one eye). Place the potato sections in the soil and cover with a mound of soil. Place the pot in a sunny location. Use a spray bottle to water your potato patch each day. Check the soil at least twice a week. Add more water if the soil is dry. Place your label in the pot.

Potato Patch Label

The ozone was discovered in 1840 by Christian Frederick Schönbein.

9 • William Henry Harrison
1841

Born: February 9, 1773
Died: April 4, 1841

William Henry Harrison was the last President born a British subject. He enjoyed morning walks and horseback riding. He also enjoyed shopping early in the morning for breakfast items. His inaugural parade featured floats with log cabins and cider barrels. During President Harrison's short term, many people asked him for jobs. He kept his pockets full of job requests.

Inaugural Parade Floats

Materials: pencil, paper, crayons, markers, glue, poster board, scissors, two empty checkbook boxes, four craft sticks, red, white, and blue ribbon

Copy, color, and cut out poster board patterns. Make two sets of wheels. Glue one apple to each cider barrel. Fold the log cabin and cider barrel. Decorate two checkbook box covers. Cut two slits in the top of each box as shown below. Insert a craft stick in each slit. Drape and glue red, white, and blue ribbons to the craft sticks. Glue one set of wheels to the sides of each box. Place the log cabin and cider barrel on a float.

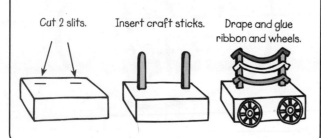

Cut 2 slits.   Insert craft sticks.   Drape and glue ribbon and wheels.

Pockets Full of Petitions

Materials: scissors, construction paper, poster board, hole punch, yarn, tape, glue, button, index cards

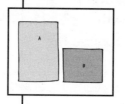
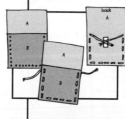
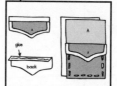

Cut a 4" x 5" construction paper pocket. Cut a 5" x 7" poster board backing. Align the bottom of the pocket and backing and punch holes along the sides and bottom of both sheets as shown. Lace yarn through the holes and secure the loose ends to the back with tape. Copy or trace, color, and cut out the pocket flap. Fold and apply glue to the tab. Attach the flap to the pocket. Glue a button on the (x). Punch two holes at the top of the backing board and attach a length of yarn for hanging. Write notes to friends or family members on index cards and place them in the pocket.

William Henry Harrison served the shortest term, one month, as President of the United States.

William Henry Harrison is the only President whose grandson, Benjamin Harrison, also became President.

The American Presidents ©2000 Monday Morning Books, Inc.

Parade Float Patterns

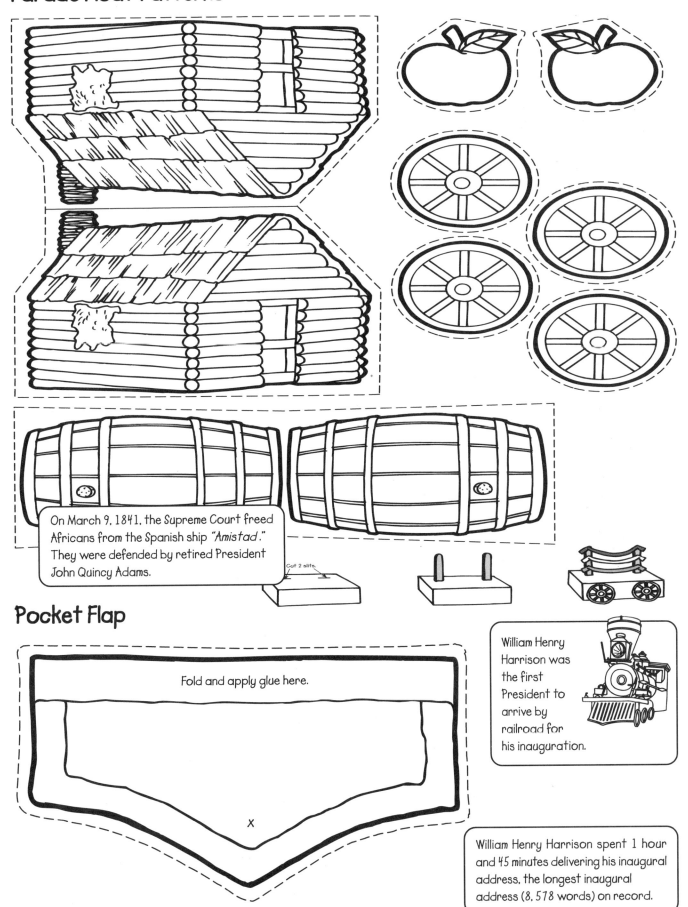

On March 9, 1841, the Supreme Court freed Africans from the Spanish ship *"Amistad."* They were defended by retired President John Quincy Adams.

Cut 2 slits.

Pocket Flap

Fold and apply glue here.

X

William Henry Harrison was the first President to arrive by railroad for his inauguration.

William Henry Harrison spent 1 hour and 45 minutes delivering his inaugural address, the longest inaugural address (8,578 words) on record.

The American Presidents ©2000 Monday Morning Books, Inc.

★ ★

Born: March 29, 1790
Died: January 18, 1862

10 • John Tyler
1841-1845

John Tyler learned to play the violin from his father. When he retired he enjoyed playing for guests. One of his favorite tunes was "Home Sweet Home." President Tyler married Julia Gardiner while in office on June 26, 1844. The First Lady was known for her lively White House entertainment, which included dancing the polka. John Tyler is best remembered for admitting Texas and Florida into the Union. Julia Gardiner Tyler was also in favor of annexing Texas. She wore the gold pen President Tyler used to sign the annexation bill on a chain as a necklace.

Texas Necklace

Materials: pencil, paper, crayons, permanent markers, scissors, glue, margarine tub lid, hole punch, gold ribbon or yellow yarn

Trace or copy, color, and cut out the Texas medallion. Glue the medallion to a margarine tub lid. Use a permanent marker to color the edge of the lid. Punch a hole and lace a length of gold ribbon or yellow yarn for a chain.

Everybody Polka

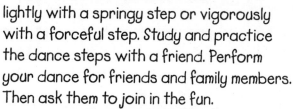

The polka is a lively folk-dance of mixed origins. Dancers are arranged or move in a circle. It can be danced lightly with a springy step or vigorously with a forceful step. Study and practice the dance steps with a friend. Perform your dance for friends and family members. Then ask them to join in the fun.

The first telegraph news dispatch was sent to the Baltimore *Patriot* on May 25, 1844.

John Tyler's second wife, Julia Gardiner, initiated playing "Hail to the Chief" at the President's entrance.

Adhesive postage stamps were first used on February 15, 1842.

Florida was admitted as the 27th state on March 3, 1845.

Family Sing-a-Long

Ask your family to join you in a weekly sing-a-long activity. Begin by singing songs that are familiar to both adults and children in your family. As your sing-a-long becomes a regular activity, introduce new songs or ask family members to make suggestions.

The American Presidents ©2000 Monday Morning Books, Inc.

Texas Medallion

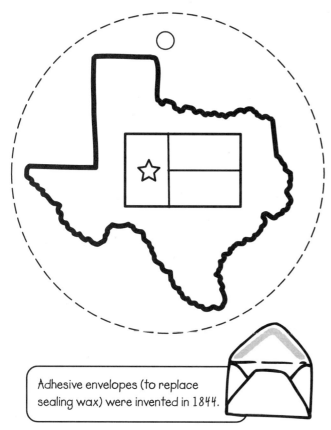

Adhesive envelopes (to replace sealing wax) were invented in 1844.

Polka Dance Steps

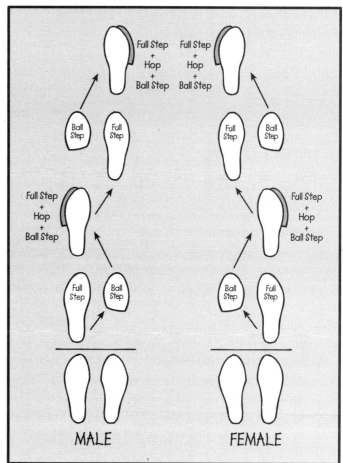

MALE   FEMALE

Animal Stamps

Both President Tyler and the First Lady, Julia Gardiner Tyler, loved animals. They kept a menagerie in the White House that included a canary named Johnny Ty and a greyhound called Le Beau.

Animal Lovers Stamp Poster

Materials: pencil, paper, crayons, markers, scissors, glue, poster board or oak tag

Draw a rough sketch of your poster on a sheet of paper. Transfer your design to a sheet of poster board. Decorate the poster with crayons, markers, magazine cutouts, glitter, and other craft supplies. Copy or draw your own animal stamps. Color, cut out, and glue the animal stamps to your poster.

Pets for the President

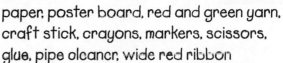

Materials:

paper, poster board, red and green yarn, craft stick, crayons, markers, scissors, glue, pipe cleaner, wide red ribbon

Trace or copy the pet and pet home patterns. Color and glue the patterns to poster board. Cut out each pattern. Punch two holes where indicated on the canary. Cut a 4" length of pipe cleaner and bend it into a "V" shape. Thread one end through each hole for legs. Glue red yarn bars on the bird cage. Glue green yarn and a craft stick to the cage to form a swing. Glue the canary to the cage and the greyhound to the dog house. Tie and glue a red ribbon to the top of each pet home.

Mount St. Helens, Washington, erupted on November 22, 1842.

Mount Rainier, Washington, erupted on November 13, 1843.

Johnny Ty and Le Beau

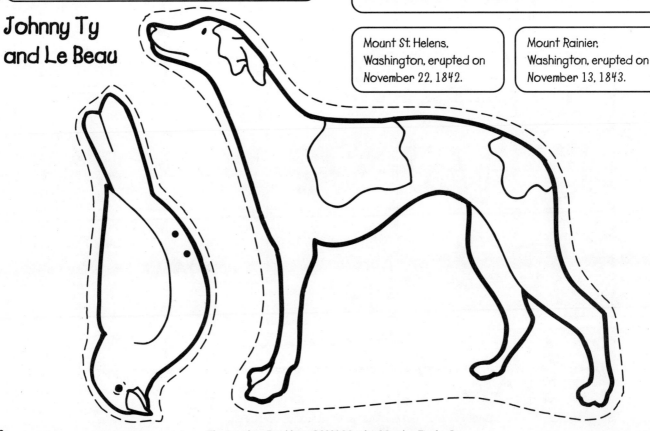

The American Presidents ©2000 Monday Morning Books, Inc.

Two-in-One Pet House

Use this pattern to make both a dog house and a bird cage. Trace each pet home separately or make two copies, one for each pet home as shown.

★ ★

11 • James Knox Polk
1845-1849

At the age of 10, James traveled from North Carolina to Tennessee in a wagon over 500 miles of rough country. In college, he enjoyed mathematics. As a young adult he enjoyed politics above all other interests. The First Lady, Sarah Childress Polk, hosted the first annual Thanksgiving dinner at the White House.

Born: November 2, 1795
Died: June 15, 1849

Life in the Original Mobile Home

Materials: construction paper, crayons, markers, scissors, glue, old magazines

Fold a sheet of construction paper in half to form a folder. Copy, color, and cut out the covered wagon patterns. Write a message on the covered wagon. Glue it to the front of the construction paper folder as shown above. Glue the supply pictures to the inside of the folder. Add pages with magazine cutouts of things you would take on a 500-mile covered wagon trip. Insert them in your folder.

A White House Thanksgiving

Materials: pencil, paper, glue, poster board, scissors, 12" x 18" construction paper, old magazines, tape

Copy or trace and decorate construction paper dinnerware. Decorate a construction paper place mat to match your dinnerware. Cut a 2" fringe on the short sides of the place mat. Glue magazine food pictures to poster board and cut out. Cut out and tape a large construction paper storage pocket to the back of your place mat. Set up your place mat and dinnerware. Then choose the foods you would serve for a White House Thanksgiving. Make two place mat and dinnerware sets. Ask a friend to play host or hostess with you.

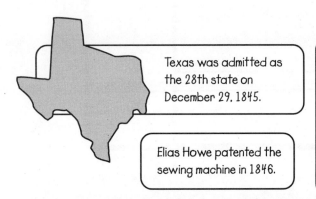

Texas was admitted as the 28th state on December 29, 1845.

Elias Howe patented the sewing machine in 1846.

Iowa was admitted as the 29th state on December 28, 1846.

Wisconsin was admitted as the 30th state on May 29, 1848.

On March 4, 1845, Samuel F.B. Morse sent the first telegraph news report of a Presidential inauguration.

The American Presidents ©2000 Monday Morning Books, Inc.

Covered Wagon Patterns

The American Medical Association was established on May 5, 1847.

Neptune was discovered in 1846 by Johann Gottfield Galle and Heinrich Ludwig d'Arrest.

Dinnerware

The American Presidents ©2000 Monday Morning Books, Inc.

★ ★

12 • Zachary Taylor
1849-1850

Born: November 24, 1784
Died: July 9, 1850

General Zachary Taylor was nicknamed "Old Rough and Ready" because of his frontier bluntness and disregard for clothes. He preferred civilian clothes and wore a battered straw hat. In 1849, the Home Department was established. The name was later changed to the Department of Interior. Its primary function was to manage the nation's natural resources. These included public lands, water, fuel, mineral,s wildlife, and the national parks system.

America's Natural Resources

Natural Resources Collage

Materials: poster board, crayons, markers, scissors, wildlife and travel magazines, glue, twigs, leaves, sand, aluminum foil, cotton balls, cellophane

Trace the outline of the United States map. Write a title or slogan on the map. Color, cut out, and glue the map on a sheet of poster board. Cut out and glue wildlife and travel magazine pictures that show America's natural resources. Add trees made from twigs and small leaves. Use cellophane for water. Use aluminum foil for metals. Color aluminum foil with a yellow marker to represent gold. Use sand for beaches and deserts. Use cotton balls for snow-capped mountains. Decorate your poster with crayons or markers.

A "Rough and Ready" Straw Hat

Materials: poster board, pencil, ruler, scissors, tape, brown grocery bag, glue, adult helper

Ask an adult to help you measure and cut out the crown, brim, and hatband. Follow the directions to assemble your hat. Tear grocery bag strips to glue to your assembled hat.

Abraham Lincoln patented inflated cylinders for bouying vessels on May 22, 1849.

Walter Hunt and Charles Rowley invented the safety pin in 1849.

Zachary Taylor's horse had the run of the White House lawn.

Making a Straw Hat

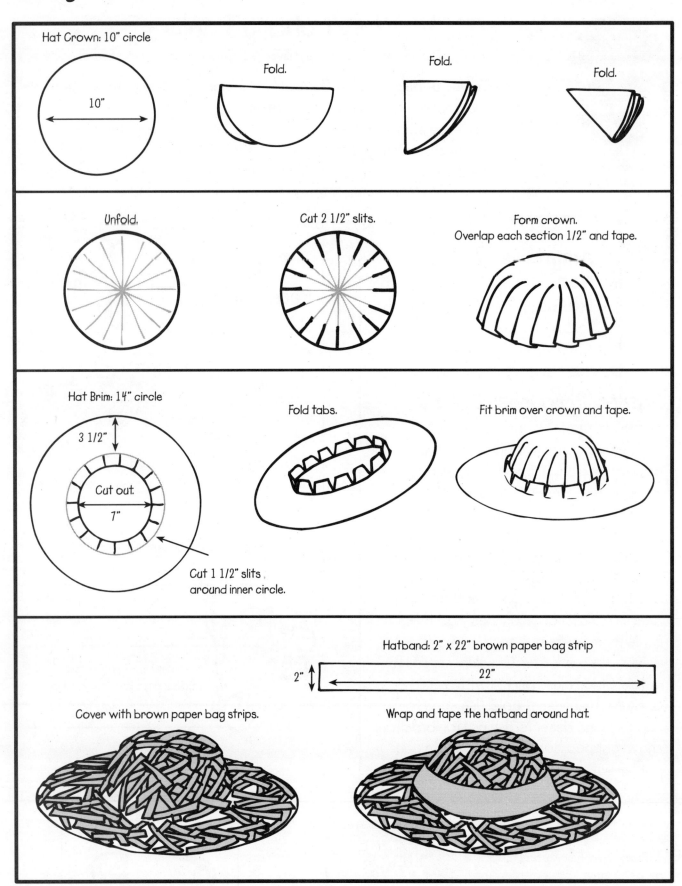

Hat Crown: 10" circle

10"

Fold.

Fold.

Fold.

Unfold.

Cut 2 1/2" slits.

Form crown.
Overlap each section 1/2" and tape.

Hat Brim: 14" circle

3 1/2"

Cut out.

7"

Cut 1 1/2" slits
around inner circle.

Fold tabs.

Fit brim over crown and tape.

Hatband: 2" x 22" brown paper bag strip

2"

22"

Cover with brown paper bag strips.

Wrap and tape the hatband around hat.

The American Presidents ©2000 Monday Morning Books, Inc.

★★★★★★★★★★★★★★★★★★★★★★★★★★★★★★★★★★★

13 • Millard Fillmore
1850-1853

Born: January 7, 1800
Died: March 8, 1874

Millard Fillmore dreamed of leaving the farm for a "career of distinction." As a young man, he used a dictionary to improve his vocabulary. Millard Fillmore had an extensive private library. He and the First Lady, Abigail Powers Fillmore, started the first permanent White House Library. Millard Fillmore spent a lot of time away from home. He and Abigail wrote many letters to each other. They wrote of both personal and political matters.

Organize a Book Fair

Materials: pencil, construction paper, poster board, crayons, markers, scissors, glue, books

Ask friends and family members to help you organize a book fair. Ask them to contribute used books to sell or trade at the fair. Copy or trace the book fair patterns. Cut out construction paper price tags to fit in the books. Make book plates and bookmarks for shoppers to trade or purchase. Make and display a poster board doorknob hanger on your door on Book Fair day.

This book belongs to

Book Fair

Keep Your Memories in Letters

Materials: pen or pencil, stationery or other writing paper, shoe box, construction paper, gift wrap, crayons, markers, scissors, glue

Cover a shoe box and lid with gift wrap or decorate with construction paper, crayons, and markers. Write about people and special events in letter format. You can write to a parent, sibling, teacher, classmate, or future friend. Write the date and city at the top of your letter. You may want to include photographs or drawings in your letters. Fold and store your letters in the shoe box.

California was admitted as the 31st state on September 9, 1850.

Book Fair Patterns

Uncle Tom's Cabin, by Harriet Beecher Stowe, was published in 1852.

The 1850 Fugitive Slave Law forced many citizens to help runaway slaves escape through the Underground Railroad to Canada.

The Capitol building was partially destroyed by fire on December 24, 1851.

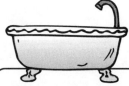

.Abigail Powers Fillmore had the first bathtub installed in the White House.

Bookmark

Doorknob hanger

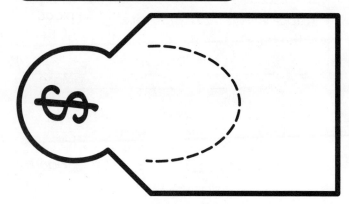

Price tag

The American Presidents ©2000 Monday Morning Books, Inc.

★ ★

14 • Franklin Pierce
1853-1857

Born: November 25, 1804
Died: October 8, 1869

Franklin Pierce was the first President born in the 19th century. He learned to read and write in a brick schoolhouse. During recess, he tutored other students. Very little was known about Franklin Pierce when he was nominated for the Presidency. This made it necessary for Franklin to put his picture on posters. On July 14, 1853, President Pierce opened the Crystal Palace Exposition in New York. It featured industrial, manufacturing, and invention displays.

Schoolhouse Writing Tablet

Materials: pencil, ruler, poster board, crayons, markers, scissors, blank or lined paper, stapler

Copy or trace and cut out a poster board schoolhouse and staple board. Color the schoolhouse. Measure and cut 5" x 5" sheets of blank or lined paper for writing. Align the staple board along one side of the writing sheets and staple to the schoolhouse as shown.

Let Me Introduce Myself

Materials: pencil, crayons, markers, photograph (optional)

Pretend you are an unknown Presidential candidate. Make a copy of the Let Me Introduce Myself poster. Draw or glue a picture of yourself on the poster. Write your name where indicated. Then write a paragraph about yourself. Include where you live, your interests, and hobbies. Mention clubs you belong to and community projects you participate in.

Crystal Palace Diorama

Materials: box with lid, scissors, glue, silver glitter, Styrofoam, toothpicks, tape, cellophane or plastic wrap, adult helper

Ask an adult to cut windows in the sides of a box and lid. Apply glue and glitter to the box and lid. Measure, cut, and place a piece of Styrofoam in the bottom of the box. Cut and tape cellophane or plastic wrap on the inside of each window. Make two copies of the invention patterns. Glue matching patterns, back to back, to toothpicks. When dry, push the toothpicks into the Styrofoam. Secure with glue. Place the cover on your Crystal Palace.

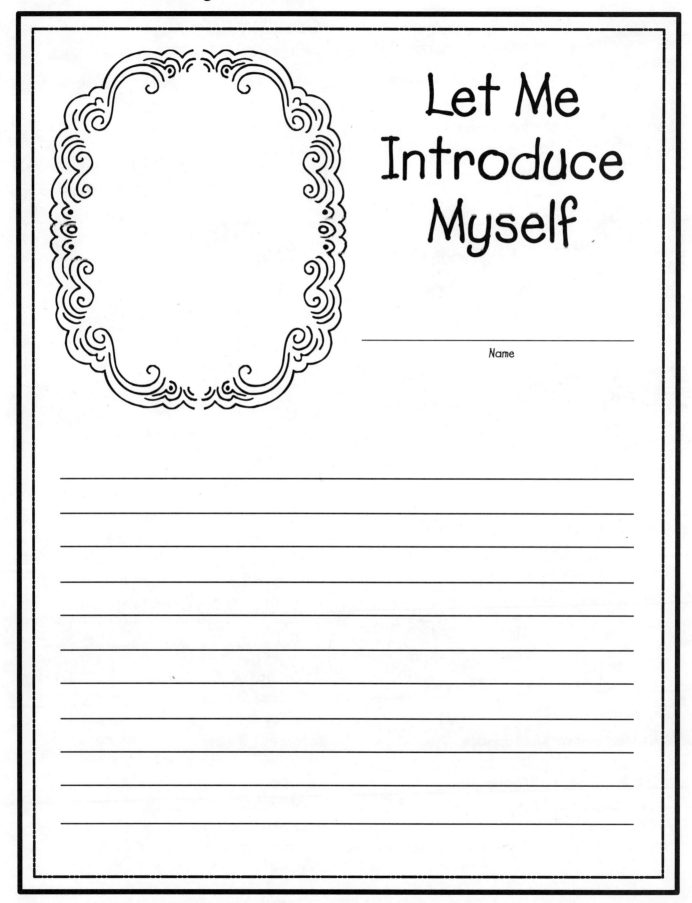

Let Me Introduce Myself

Name

The American Presidents ©2000 Monday Morning Books, Inc.

19th-Century Inventions

1815
Davy's miner's lamp
Sir Humphrey Davy

1816
Kaleidoscope
Dr. David Brewster

1822
Accordion
Friedrich L. Buschmann

1831
Reaping machine
Cyrus McCormick

1834
Adhesive postage stamp
James Chalmers

1848
Chewing gum
John Curtis

1851
Ophthalmoscope
Herman von Helmholtz

1856
Foot seeder
G. A. Meacham

1858
Pencil with attached eraser
Hyman Lipman

1857
Elevator
E. G. Otis

1862
Rubber stamps
John Leighton

1863
Roller skates
J.L. Plimpton

1865
Western 10 gallon hat
John B. Stetson

1867
Typewriter
Christopher L. Sholes

1868
Lawn mower
Amariah M. Hills

1871
Penny farthing
James Starley

1876
Telephone
Alexander Graham Bell

1878
Phonograph
Thomas Alva Edison

1879
Light bulb
Thomas Edison

1884
Fountain pen
Louis E. Waterman

Brick Schoolhouse

It cost $322 to build and take down Franklin Pierce's inaugural grandstand. This included pay for 16 extra policemen.

In 1856, G. A. Meacham invented the foot seeder. He designed it for farmers to fasten to their boots to speed up planting seeds.

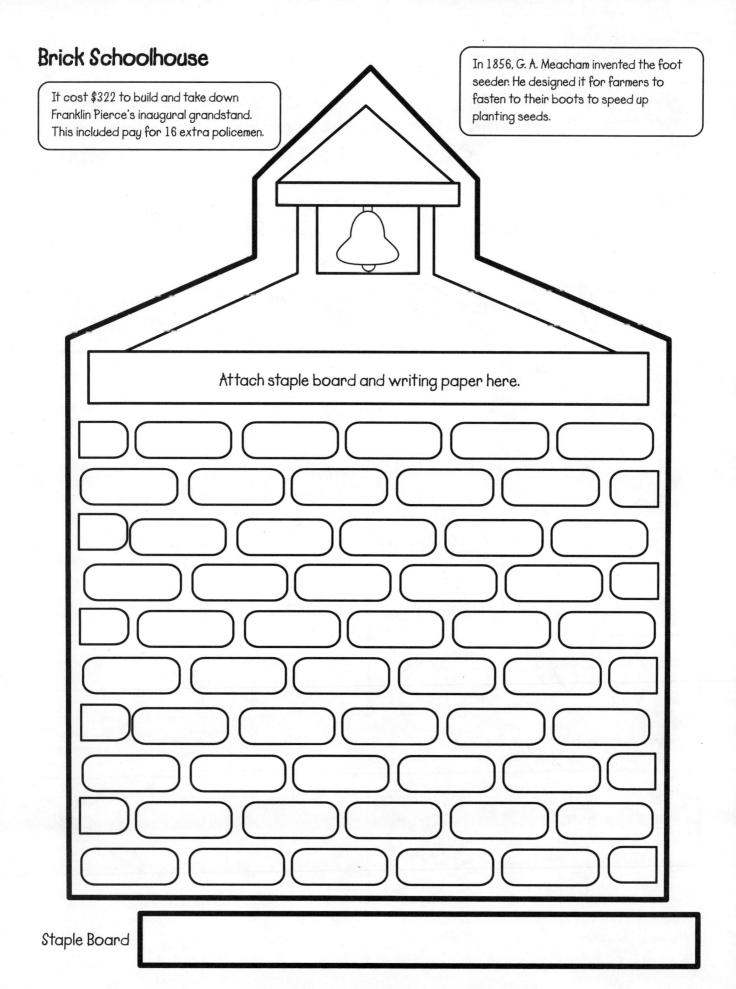

Attach staple board and writing paper here.

Staple Board

The American Presidents ©2000 Monday Morning Books, Inc.

★ ★

15 • James Buchanan
1857-1861

Born: April 23, 1791
Died: June 1, 1868

James Buchanan enjoyed reading. Extravagant foods were served at President Buchanan's inaugural ball. There was enough to feed 6,000 guests. In 1860, President Buchanan was host to the future Edward VII, the Prince of Wales. The Prince planted a buckeye tree at Mount Vernon. It did not survive. However, in 1919, a second Prince, later the Duke of Windsor, planted an English yew that survived.

A Colossal Banquet Menu

Materials: poster board, crayons, markers, scissors, glue, cooking magazines, grocery store ads

What's on the menu?

Create a giant menu of all your favorite foods to display in your home kitchen. Copy the poster shown or design your own. Use crayons and markers to decorate the menu. Copy, color, cut out, and add food patterns to your poster. Or use cutout food pictures from grocery advertisements and magazines.

Banquet Math

Materials: paper, pencil

$$125 \overline{)6,000}$$
$$6,000 \div 125 =$$

The foods served at President Buchanan's inaugural ball included 400 gallons–oysters, 60 saddles–mutton (sheep), 4 saddles–venison (deer), 125 tongues, 75 hams, 500 quarts–chicken salad, 500 quarts–jelly, 1,200 quarts–ice cream

Can you solve these problems?

- If each guest ate $1/2$ cup of chicken salad, how many quarts would be left? (4 cups = 1 quart)
- How many tablespoons of jelly are in 500 quarts? (16 tablespoons = 1 cup.)
- How many cups of ice cream could each guest eat?

Create more math problems to work with friends and family members.

A Tree Collage

Materials: pencil, poster board, scissors, glue, glitter, crayons, markers, twigs, straws, toothpicks, gift wrap, wallpaper scraps, construction paper, craft tissue, magazines, aluminum foil, small leaves, cotton balls

Copy or trace the tree trunk onto poster board. Glue twigs, straws, or toothpicks to form the trunk and branches. Cut out and glue leaves and blossoms from the materials listed above. Use these craft materials to create your unique tree collage. Decorate the rest of your picture.

Food

The American Presidents ©2000 Monday Morning Books, Inc.

Tree Trunk

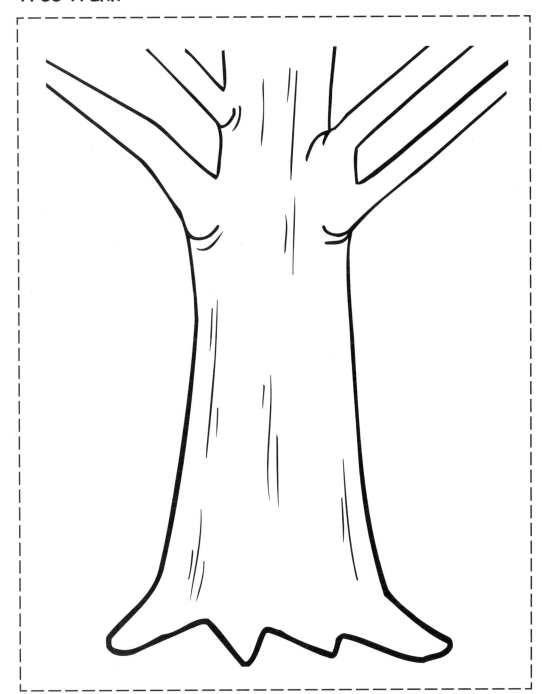

Minnesota was admitted as the 32nd state on May 11, 1858.

Oregon was admitted as the 33rd state on February 14, 1859.

Kansas was admitted as the 34th state on January 29, 1861.

The Pony Express began on April 3, 1860.

The National Association of Baseball Players was organized in 1858.

John P. Charlton created the postcard in 1861.

★ ★

Born: February 12, 1809
Died: April 15, 1865

16 • Abraham Lincoln
1861–1865

Abraham Lincoln enjoyed reading, the theater, and telling jokes. One of his favorite books was *Robinson Crusoe*. Lincoln's stovepipe hat was one of his trademarks. President Lincoln was shot and killed in 1865. The contents of his pockets on the night he died remained guarded for more than 100 years. In 1976 the contents were made known. They included two pairs of spectacles, a pocket knife, watch fob, wallet, pencil, Confederate five-dollar bill, and newspaper articles.

Make a Stovepipe Hat

Materials: black construction paper, pencil, ruler, scissors, tape, 2"-wide black ribbon

Measure and cut a 10" black construction paper circle. Cut out a 4" circle from the center. This will form the brim of your hat. Cut 1" tabs around the inner circle as pictured in the diagram. Fold all the tabs in the same direction. Measure, cut, and roll a 10" x 22" sheet of black construction paper for the crown of your hat. Assemble the crown and brim as shown and secure with tape. Cut a 23"-long ribbon hatband and glue it around your hat.

A Personal Time Capsule

Materials: box with lid, crayons, markers, scissors, glue, gift wrap, construction paper, magazines, newspaper, spray lacquer, an adult helper, items you will put in your time capsule, pen, paper

Decorate a shoe box or other storage container with crayons, markers, magazine cutouts, and other craft supplies. Ask an adult to help you spray the box with lacquer. Remember to spray in a well-ventilated area. Collect items to put in your time capsule. Write something about each item on a sheet of paper. Place all the items in the box. Write the date, city, and state on the outside of the box. Put it away for at least one year.

The Emancipation Proclamation was issued on January 1, 1863.

At age 18, Abraham Lincoln operated a ferry boat.

The American Presidents ©2000 Monday Morning Books, Inc.

★ ★ ★ ★ ★ ★ ★ ★ ★ ★ ★ ★ ★ ★ ★ ★   ★ ★ ★ ★ ★ ★ ★ ★ ★ ★ ★ ★ ★ ★ ★ ★

Lincoln used his top hat as a portable office. He kept important papers in its crown.

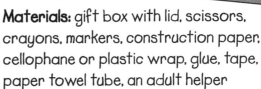

Top Hat Memo Holder

Materials: small cereal box, poster board, crayons, markers, scissors, glue, pencil, index cards

Cut a small cereal box in half to form a memo holder. Cover the box with construction paper. Copy or trace and color a poster board hat. Cut a slit along the dotted line. Apply glue to the back of the hat along the side and bottom edges only. Attach it to the cereal box. Place a pencil and blank index cards in the box. Use the slit pocket to leave reminder notes for yourself or messages for friends.

One parade float at Lincoln's inauguration carried 34 girls. Each one represented one of the states. There was also a military parade.

A Shadow Box for Lincoln

Materials: gift box with lid, scissors, crayons, markers, construction paper, cellophane or plastic wrap, glue, tape, paper towel tube, an adult helper

Ask an adult to help you cut a window in the top of a gift box. Decorate the outside of the box. Measure, cut, and glue construction paper inside the box. Copy or trace, color, and cut out the shadow box patterns. Cut a paper towel tube in half lengthwise. Cut a piece of a tube half to glue to the back of each shadow box pattern. Assemble the patterns in the box and secure with glue or tape. Tape a sheet of cellophane or plastic wrap to the inside of the box lid window. Place the lid on your shadow box.

Top Hat

Cut.

Cut.

Shadow Box Patterns

In 1863, Eddie Cuthbert, of the Philadelphia Keystones, was the first to steal a base in baseball. The game was against the Brooklyn Atlantics.

Abraham Lincoln was the first President to wear a beard.

President Lincoln delivered his Gettysburg address on November 19, 1863.

Roller skating was introduced to America in 1863.

Abraham Lincoln was the first President to obtain a patent.

West Virginia was admitted as the 35th state on June 19, 1863.

Nevada was admitted as the 36th state on October 31, 1864.

Lincoln Memorial

The American Presidents ©2000 Monday Morning Books, Inc.

★ ★

17 • Andrew Johnson

1865-1869

Born: December 29, 1808
Died: July 31, 1875

Andrew Johnson enjoyed playing checkers and the circus. He worked as a tailor and boasted he "did good work." The 13th and 14th amendments were passed during President Johnson's term in office. The United States purchased Alaska from Russia for more than $7,000,000. There were few funds to manage the White House. Linen furniture covers and flowers were used to freshen the rooms. And cows on the lawn provided milk for the family.

Circus Checkers

Materials: crayons, markers, scissors, glue, poster board, old checkerboard, envelope

Make a copy of the circus checkers. Color and glue the checkers to a sheet of poster board. Cut the checkers apart. Set up a game with an old checkerboard and your circus checkers. Ask a friend to play one, or two, or three games with you. Store your checkers in an envelope.

A History Quilt for Andrew Johnson

13th Amendment

14th Amendment

A Presidential History Quilt

Materials: paper, pencil, crayons, markers, scissors, glue

Copy, color, and cut out the quilt patterns. Assemble and glue the patterns on a sheet of poster board. Use a marker to draw stitch lines around each pattern. Draw a stitch border around the poster board to complete President Johnson's History Quilt.

The 13th amendment to the Constitution abolished slavery. The 14th amendment protected the rights of citizens.

Andrew Johnson was the first President to receive a visit from a queen, Queen Emma of the Sandwich Islands (Hawaii).

The Civil War ended on May 26, 1865.

Andrew Johnson never attended school. He learned how to write when he was 17.

Circus Checkers

Use the checkerboard on page 34.

 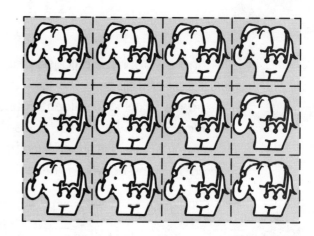

Miss Smith of Australia developed the Granny Smith apple in 1868.

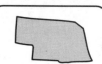

Nebraska was admitted as the 37th state on March 1, 1867.

Quilt Patterns

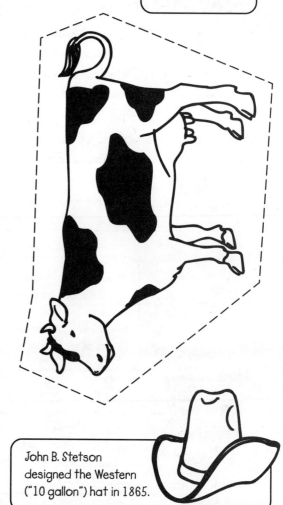

John B. Stetson designed the Western ("10 gallon") hat in 1865.

The American Presidents ©2000 Monday Morning Books, Inc.

Quilt Patterns

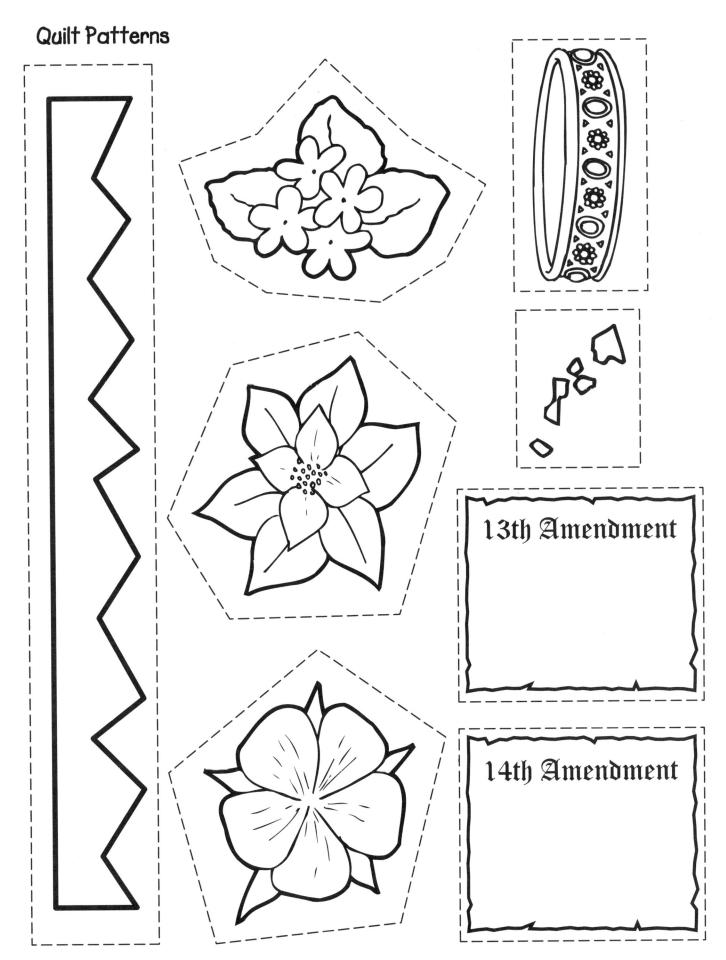

13th Amendment

14th Amendment

★★

18 • Ulysses Simpson Grant
1869-1877

Born: April 27, 1822
Died: July 23, 1885

Ulysses Simpson Grant enjoyed drawing and painting. He was very good in math and also had a talent for handling horses. Ulysses was a Union general in the Civil War. After his presidency, Grant began writing his *Memoirs* in 1884 and finished in 1885 before he died. His book earned his family more than $400,000 in royalties.

Memoir Storyboard Mural

Materials: pencil, paper, crayons, markers, scissors, glue, poster board

Make several copies of the storyboard pattern. Draw pictures in the storyboard windows that reflect your personal experiences. Include drawings of special events, birthdays, vacations, sports, and grandparents. Write a brief description under each drawing. Make additional storyboard sheets as you need to. Cut out and glue your storyboard pages to a large sheet of poster board. Write a title at the top of the poster board. Add your name in the lower right-hand corner.

Bean Bag Horse Race

Materials: a clean old sock, felt, scissors, needle and thread, raw rice or beans, permanent marker, rubber band, masking tape, open floor space, friends

Trace or copy the bean bag horse patterns. Follow the directions to assemble your bean bag horse. Measure and mark racing lanes on the floor with masking tape. Mark the finish line in each lane with a masking tape X. To play: From the starting line, players toss their bean bag horse toward the X in their racing lane. The horse closest to the finish line wins the race.

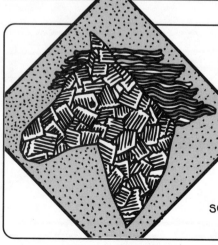

Equine Collage

Materials: scissors, glue, sandpaper, newspaper, yarn, poster board

Glue torn sandpaper to a poster board square. Copy or trace, and cut out the horse pattern. Glue torn newspaper to the horse. When the glue has dried, trim away the excess newspaper. Glue the horse to the sandpaper square. Add a yarn mane to the horse with glue.

The American Presidents ©2000 Monday Morning Books, Inc.

Storyboard

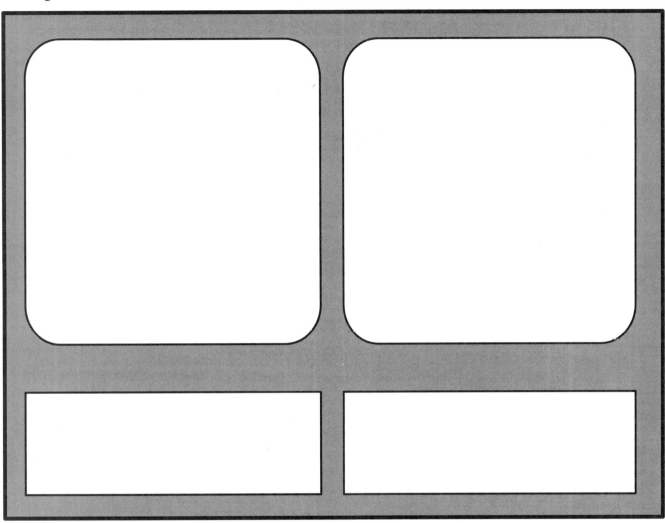

Bean Bag Horse Patterns

Cut two felt ears and a mane. Fold and stitch the bottom of each ear to the heel of a sock. Cut fringe on one side of the mane and attach with glue as shown. Fill the sock with uncooked rice or beans. Wrap a rubber band around the open end. Use a permanent marker to add eyes, a nose, and a mouth.

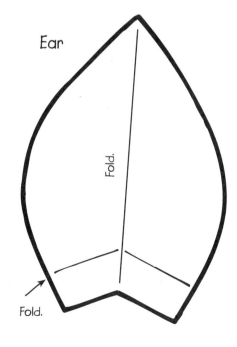

Ear

Fold.

Fold.

1. 2. 3.

Mane

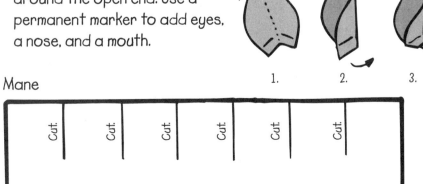

Cut. Cut. Cut. Cut. Cut. Cut.

Horse Template

Colorado was admitted as the 38th state on August 1, 1876.

It was so cold during President Grant's second inaugural ball that the guests danced with their coats on.

David Kalakaua of the Sandwich Islands (Hawaii), was the first reigning king to visit the United States.

Encouraged by Mark Twain, President Grant wrote a book about his life. Grant's book is still considered one of the all-time best-selling books.

The American Presidents ©2000 Monday Morning Books, Inc.

★ ★

19 • Rutherford Birchard Hayes
1877-1881

Born: October 4, 1822
Died: January 17, 1893

As a child, Rutherford Birchard Hayes enjoyed making cider at the family farm. He was a champion speller and had an incredible memory for names and faces. Lucy Webb Ware Hayes was nicknamed "Lemonade Lucy" because she only served lemonade and soft drinks at White House receptions. Mrs. Hayes was responsible for the annual Easter egg roll on the White House lawn.

Concentration Eggs

Materials: pencil, poster board, crayons, markers, scissors

Make seven poster board copies of the egg cards. Color and cut apart the cards. Write the name of each President and the numbers 1-42 on separate egg cards. Invite one to three friends to play with you. You must match the number to the President, so study the chronology of the Presidents. Shuffle the cards and place them all face down on a flat surface. In turn, each player turns over two cards. If there is a match, the player keeps the cards and continues to play. If there is no match, the next player takes a turn. The player with the most cards wins.

An Egg Forest for the President

Materials: paper, pencil, crayons, markers, stickers, sequins, cellophane, ribbon, yarn, glue, scissors, glitter, hole punch, pushpins

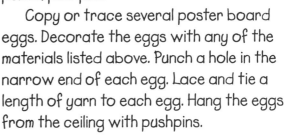

Copy or trace several poster board eggs. Decorate the eggs with any of the materials listed above. Punch a hole in the narrow end of each egg. Lace and tie a length of yarn to each egg. Hang the eggs from the ceiling with pushpins.

The first Presidential phone call took place between President Hayes and Alexander Graham Bell in 1877. President Hayes listened through receiver shaped like a bobbin.

Lemonade and Mulled Cider

Materials: apple cider, cloves, cinnamon stick, water, lemon juice, sugar, an adult helper

Cider:
Ask an adult to warm apple cider, 2 or 3 cloves, and 1 cinnamon stick (do not boil).
Lemonade: 1 cup water
3 to 4 tablespoons sugar
1 1/2 tablespoons lemon juice
Ask an adult to boil water and sugar for 2 minutes. Chill the syrup and add the lemon juice.

Egg Cards

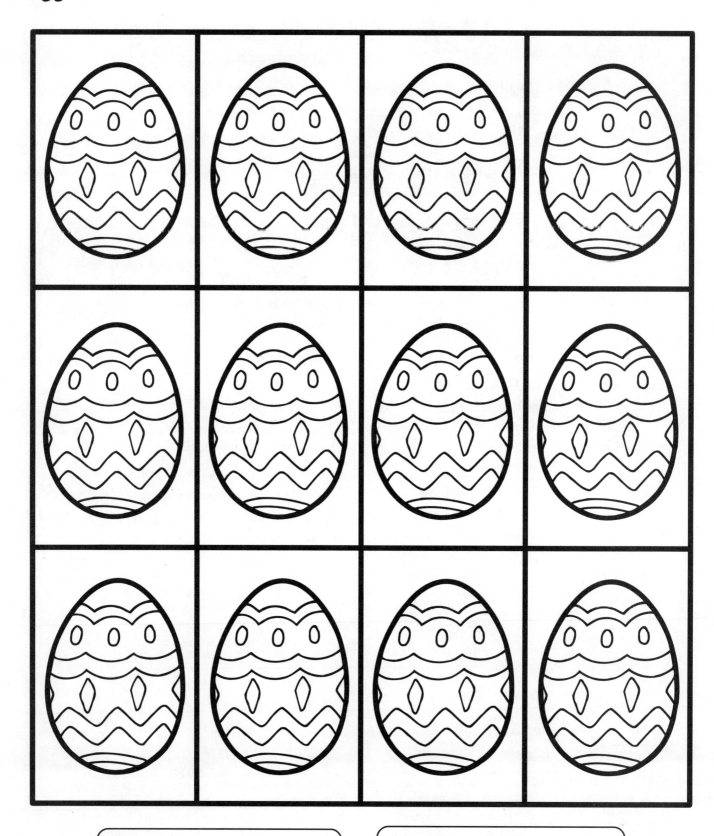

Thomas Alva Edison obtained a patent for the phonograph on February 19, 1878.

Alexander Graham Bell installed the first telephone in the White House.

The American Presidents ©2000 Monday Morning Books, Inc.

Egg

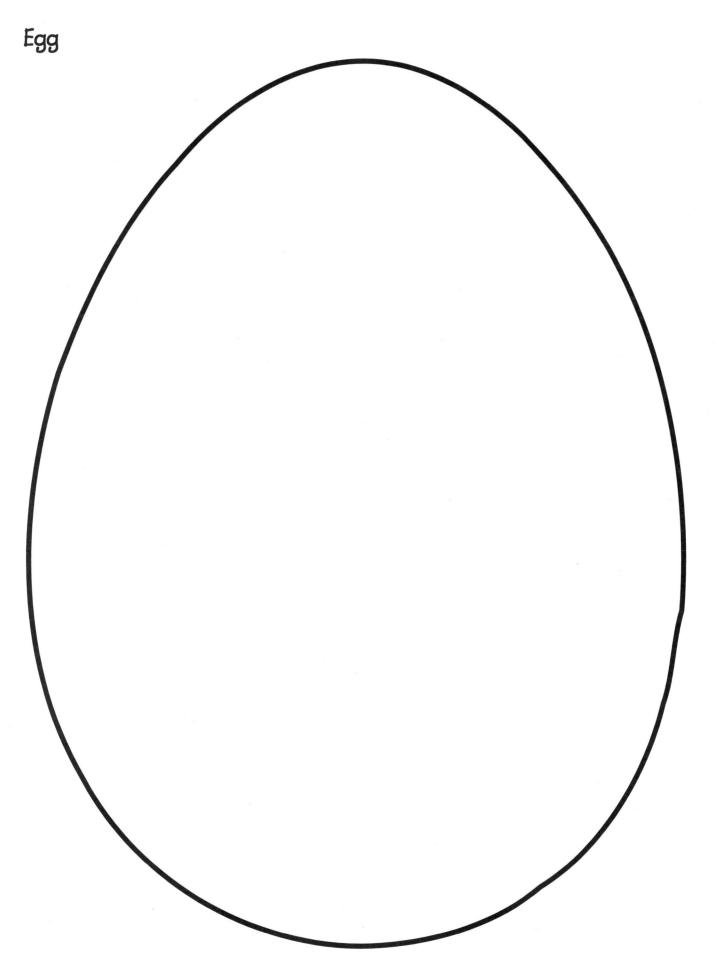

★ ★

20 • James Abram Garfield

1881

James Garfield dreamed of becoming a sailor. He often read stories of sea adventures. He also enjoyed playing whist, an early form of bridge. The First Lady, Lucretia "Crete" Rudolph Garfield, spent most of her time at the Library of Congress. She enjoyed reading about White House history.

Born: November 19, 1831
Died: September 19, 1881

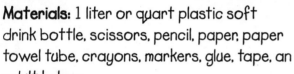

Ship in a Bottle

Materials: 1 liter or quart plastic soft drink bottle, scissors, pencil, paper, paper towel tube, crayons, markers, glue, tape, an adult helper

Ask an adult to help you cut a hinged window in a plastic soft drink bottle as shown here. Use markers to draw waves on the sides of the bottle. Copy, color, and cut out the ship. Fold the ship in half and glue it in the bottom of the bottle. Cut a paper towel tube in half lengthwise. Glue the two halves together to form a stand as shown. Place the bottle in the stand.

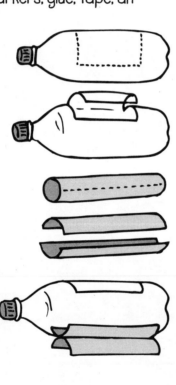

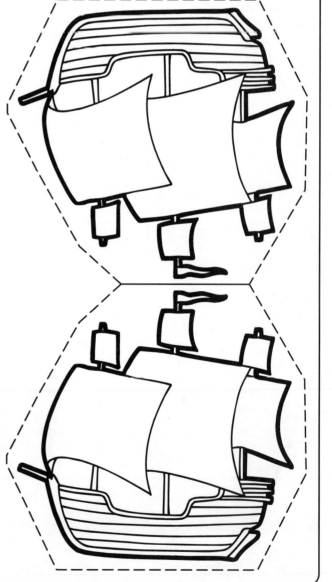

President Garfield was left-handed.

Garfield's inaugural ball was held at the Smithsonian Institution.

The American Red Cross was organized on May 21, 1881.

The American Presidents ©2000 Monday Morning Books, Inc.

★ ★

Ocean Life Mobile

Materials: shoe box lid, scissors, yarn, construction paper, crayons, markers, glue, stapler, adult helper, hole punch

Copy or trace the ocean life patterns. Color, cut out, and glue each one to a construction paper shape. Cut and staple a length of yarn to each ornament. Ask an adult to cut a window in the top of a shoe box lid. This will be your mobile frame. Decorate the frame. Punch seven holes along the long sides and three holes along the short sides of the lid. Lace and tie a length of yarn through the hole in the center of each side. Gather and tie the ends in a knot. Lace and tie the ornaments through the remaining holes.

Ocean Life Patterns

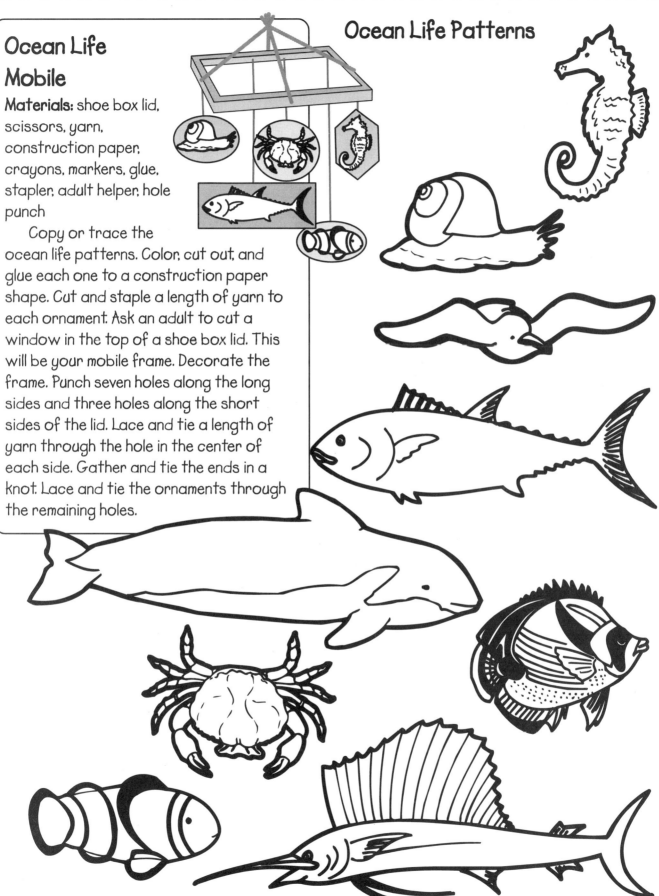

Ocean Life Patterns

The American Presidents ©2000 Monday Morning Books, Inc.

★ ★

21 • Chester Alan Arthur
1881-1885

Born: October 5, 1829
Died: November 18, 1886

Chester Alan Arthur enjoyed fishing and hunting. He also enjoyed dressing well. Sometimes he changed his clothes several times a day. President Arthur entertained White House guests at formal dinners. Bouquets of roses were given to the women and boutonnieres to the men. He also had the White House redecorated by Louis Comfort Tiffany, famous for his stained glass creations.

Stained Glass Roses

Materials: plastic wrap, permanent markers, masking tape, poster board

Cover an 8" x 12" sheet of poster board with plastic wrap. Secure the top and bottom of the plastic wrap to the back of the poster board. Make a copy of the stained glass roses design. Slide it between the plastic wrap and poster board. Use permanent markers to trace and color the design. When you are done, remove the design sheet. Secure the sides of the plastic wrap to the back of the board.

Circle of Roses

Materials: paper, crayons, markers, scissors, glue, plastic coffee can lid, hole punch, yarn, ribbon

Trace or copy, color, and cut several roses. Glue the roses to the inside of a coffee can lid. Use a permanent marker to color the edge of the lid. Punch a hole in the lid. Lace and tie a length of yarn through the hole for hanging. Tie a bow and glue it over the hole.

Stained Glass Roses

 The American Presidents ©2000 Monday Morning Books, Inc.

★ ★

22 and 24 • Grover Cleveland
1885-1889 • 1893-1897

Born: March 18, 1837
Died: June 24, 1908

Grover Cleveland understood the value of using time wisely. At the age of nine, he wrote an essay stating, "If we expect to become great and good men and be respected and esteemed by our friends we must improve our time when we are young." He enjoyed playing cribbage and fishing. On October 28, 1886, Frédédric-Auguste Bartholdi unveiled the Statue of Liberty in New York's harbor. The 151-foot tall, 225-ton statue continues to stand on Liberty Island.

An Angler's Planning Calendar

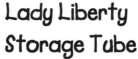

Materials: pencil, paper, scissors, glue, poster board, clear contact paper, hole punch, yarn, erasable crayon or marker

Copy or trace the calendar patterns. Glue the patterns to a sheet of poster board. Cover the entire calendar with clear contact paper and trim the edges. Punch holes and tie on a yarn hanger. Write in the month and days. Then fill in important dates and events to remember.

Lady Liberty Storage Tube

Materials: pencil, paper, crayons, markers, scissors, glue, construction paper, chip can

Copy or trace and color the Statue of Liberty pattern. Cut the bottom edge of pattern A and the top edge of pattern B, overlap, and glue both pieces onto a sheet of construction paper. When dry, cut out the statue along the dotted lines. Wrap construction paper around a chip can. Glue the statue to the can and allow to dry. Store pencils, paint brushes, markers, and rulers in your Lady Liberty storage tube.

Lady Liberty Foil Sculpture

Materials: three different size jar lids, glue, paper towel tube, aluminum foil, an adult helper

Glue the jar lids together to form a pedestal. Pinch one end of a paper towel tube and secure it with tape as shown. Crumple and wrap aluminum foil around the entire tube. Have an adult help you form a head and arms as you continue wrapping foil to your sculpture. Pinch crown spikes around the head. Glue the finished sculpture to the jar lid pedestal.

Planning Calendar

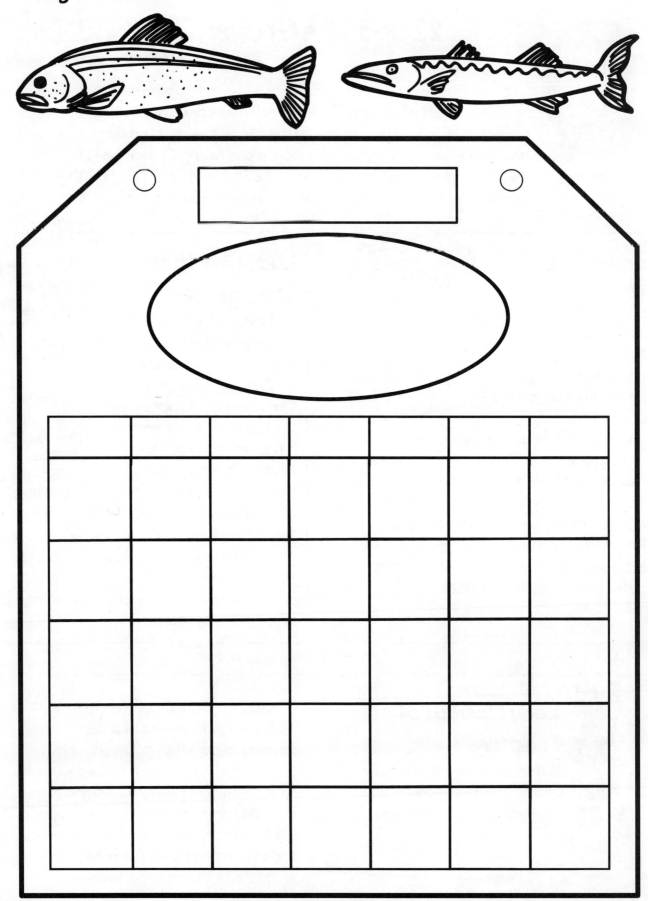

 The American Presidents ©2000 Monday Morning Books, Inc.

Statue of Liberty

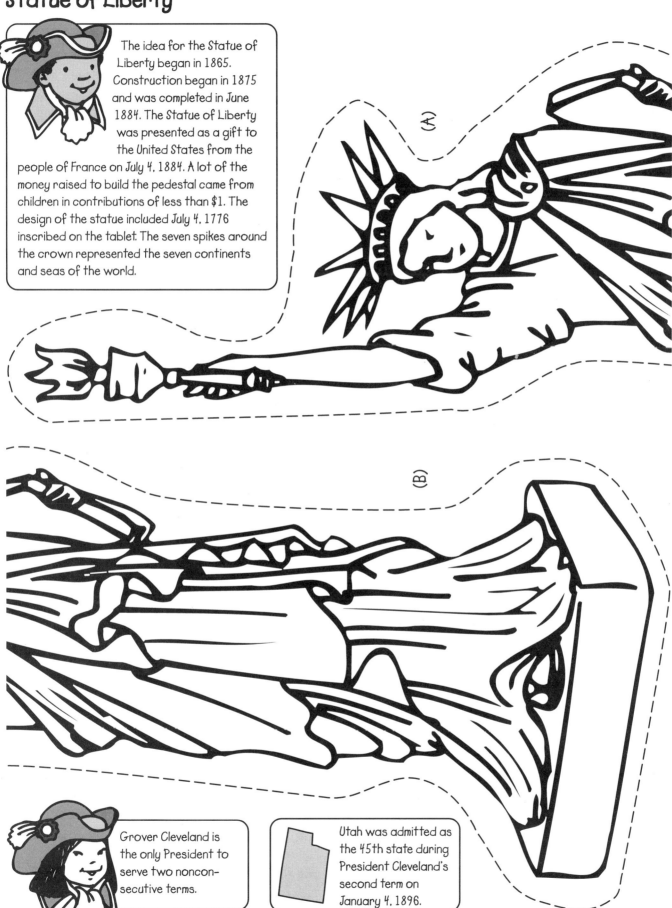

The idea for the Statue of Liberty began in 1865. Construction began in 1875 and was completed in June 1884. The Statue of Liberty was presented as a gift to the United States from the people of France on July 4, 1884. A lot of the money raised to build the pedestal came from children in contributions of less than $1. The design of the statue included July 4, 1776 inscribed on the tablet. The seven spikes around the crown represented the seven continents and seas of the world.

(A)

(B)

Grover Cleveland is the only President to serve two noncon-secutive terms.

Utah was admitted as the 45th state during President Cleveland's second term on January 4, 1896.

★ ★

23 • Benjamin Harrison
1889-1893

Born: August 20, 1833
Died: March 13, 1901

Benjamin Harrison enjoyed country life. President Harrison started the custom of flying the flag from all public buildings. Oklahoma was opened to settlers in 1889. The First Lady, Caroline Scott Harrison, introduced the custom of using orchids in the White House. Mrs. Harrison was a painter. She directed china painting classes while in the White House. She started the White House china collection. It was also her suggestion that a Christmas tree be set up in the White House.

The China Cabinet

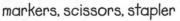

Materials: poster board, pencil, construction paper, crayons, markers, scissors, stapler

Trace or copy the china cabinet patterns. Color and cut out a poster board front and back cover. Read about each President. Use crayons and markers to decorate the plate, cup, and saucer to reflect each President's personality. Name each set of china and write the name in the box at the bottom of the page. Bind your pages between the covers and staple to form a book.

Race to Oklahoma

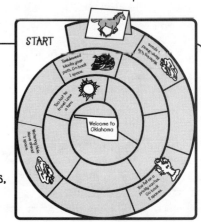

Materials: poster board, pencil, crayons, markers, scissors, die

Trace and transfer the game board onto poster board. Color and cut out the game board. Copy or trace, color, and cut out the horse game markers. Fold the game markers in half so they will stand alone. Invite a friend or two to join you in a Race to Oklahoma. To play: In turn, each player rolls a die and moves the number of spaces indicated on the die. The first player to reach Oklahoma wins.

North Dakota was admitted as the 39th state on November 2, 1889.

South Dakota was admitted as the 40th state on November 2, 1889.

Montana was admitted as the 41st state on November 8, 1889.

Washington was admitted as the 42nd state on November 11, 1889.

Idaho was admitted as the 43rd state on July 3, 1890.

Wyoming was admitted as the 44th state on July 10, 1890.

The American Presidents ©2000 Monday Morning Books, Inc.

Game Board

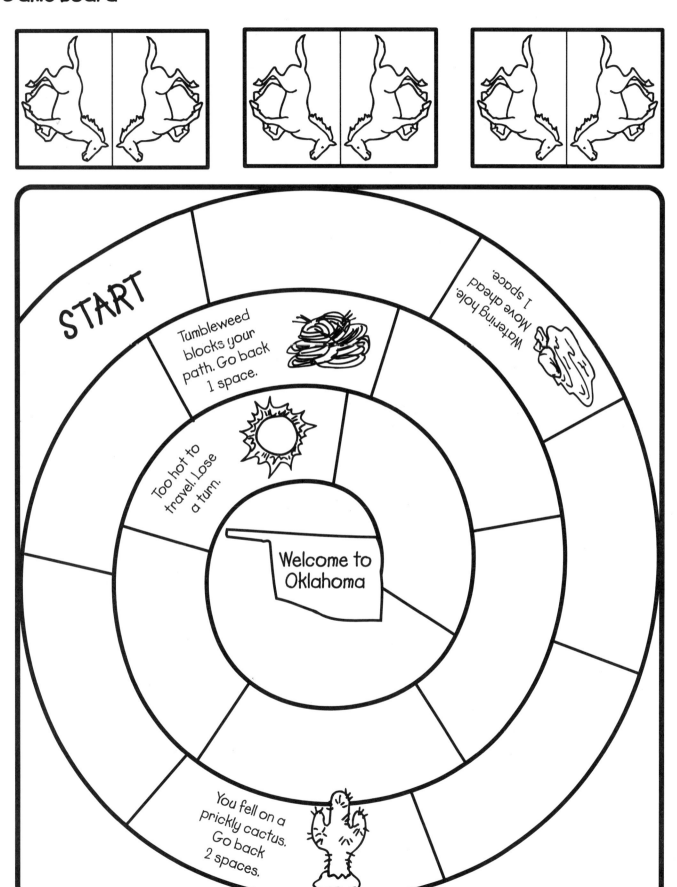

START

Tumbleweed blocks your path. Go back 1 space.

Watering hole. Move ahead 1 space.

Too hot to travel. Lose a turn.

Welcome to Oklahoma

You fell on a prickly cactus. Go back 2 spaces.

China Cabinet Cover

The American Presidents ©2000 Monday Morning Books, Inc.

China Cabinet Page

25 • William McKinley

1897–1901

Born: January 29, 1843
Died: September 14, 1901

William McKinley enjoyed outdoor activities, including ice-skating. He also liked the theater. One of William's favorite plays was *Rip Van Winkle*. He wore a red carnation for good luck during political campaigns. This prompted Ohio, McKinley's home state, to designate the scarlet carnation as the state flower. Mrs. McKinley made thousands of crocheted slippers, which she gave away to friends and acquaintances. The first automobile show was held in New York City during William McKinley's Presidency.

Red Carnation Sculptures

Materials: red craft tissue, pipe cleaners, corrugated board, black construction paper, scissors, glue, white paint, brush, long carpenter's nail, imagination

Paint a sheet of corrugated board with white paint. Allow the paint to dry. Lightly draw an outline or rough sketch of your design on the board. Carefully use a nail to punch holes 1" apart all over your design. Cut 5" red craft tissue squares. Fold each sheet like an accordion as shown below. Fold the accordion in half. Then cut and wrap a pipe cleaner around the folded end of the accordion. Twist the excess pipe cleaner into a needle. Fluff the craft tissue to look like a carnation. Push the pipe cleaner end of your carnation through a hole in the board. Continue adding carnations until your design is completely covered. Cut and glue black construction paper features or buttons if needed.

Car Show 2000

Materials: pencil, paper, crayons, markers, paint, brush, various size boxes, construction paper, poster board, jar lids, empty thread spools, cotton balls, pipe cleaners, craft sticks, buttons, cellophane or plastic wrap, aluminum foil, toothpicks, tape, hole punch, glitter, paint markers, scissors

Use a marker to draw a border around a sheet of poster board. Write Car Show 2000 at the top of the board. Copy and cut out a construction paper Model T car. Color, decorate, and glue the car to your poster. Ask friends and relatives to join you in making cars to display. Set up a work station where everyone can share the supplies.

The American Presidents ©2000 Monday Morning Books, Inc.

Model T

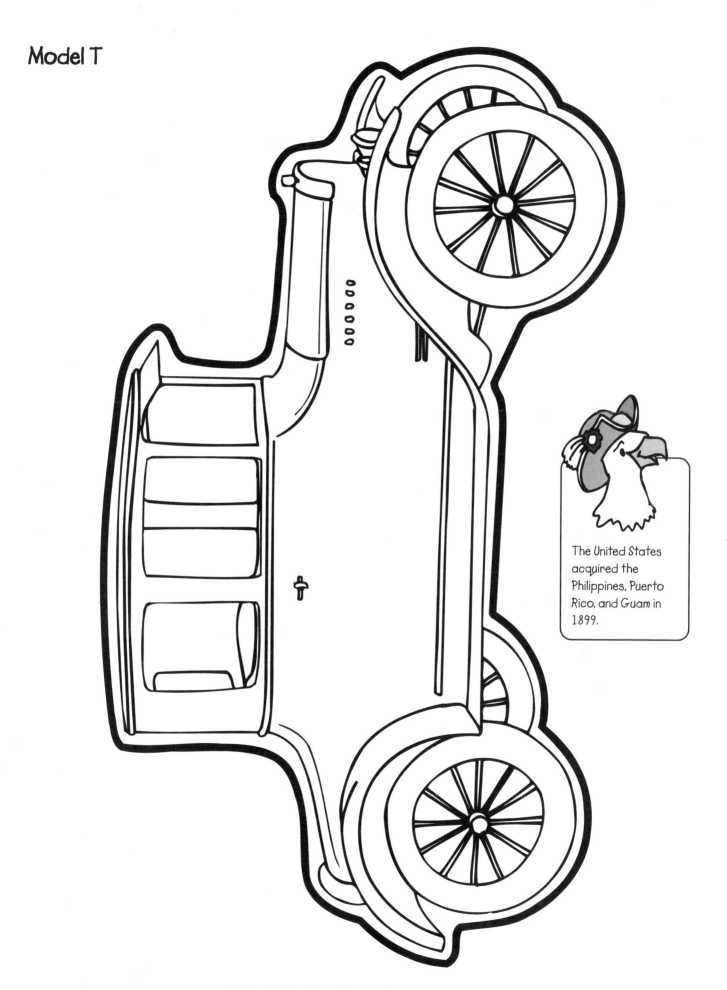

The United States acquired the Philippines, Puerto Rico, and Guam in 1899.

★ ★

26 • Theodore Roosevelt
1901–1909

Born: October 27, 1858
Died: January 6, 1919

Young Theodore wanted to be a zoologist. President Roosevelt loved children. He often took time for story telling. The toy teddy bear was named for Theodore Roosevelt. Edith Kermit Carow Roosevelt had a great love for the arts. She invited artists, musicians, and authors to visit at the White House. She also created a portrait gallery of the First Ladies. Theodore Roosevelt loved being President.

America's First Ladies Portrait Gallery

Materials: pencil, construction paper, crayons, markers, scissors, photograph, tape

Copy or trace the frame below onto construction paper. Decorate the frame with crayons or markers. Cut out the window along the dotted lines. Fold the frame. Position and tape a photograph to the back of the window. Fold the tab and secure with tape.

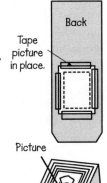

Back

Tape picture in place.

Picture

Bears for Theodore

Materials: pencil, paper, crayons, markers, scissors, glue

Copy or trace the bears and bows. Color and cut out the patterns. Attach the bows with glue as shown above. Write a message on each bear.

Portrait Frame

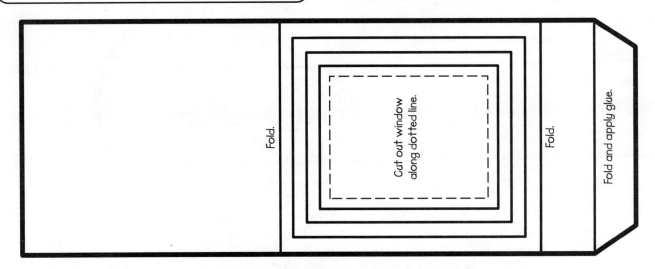

Fold.

Cut out window along dotted line.

Fold.

Fold and apply glue.

The American Presidents ©2000 Monday Morning Books, Inc.

Bears

The American Presidents ©2000 Monday Morning Books, Inc.

At the age of nine, Theodore wrote a paper entitled "The Natural History of Insects." He and two cousins also established the Roosevelt Museum of Natural History with a variety of specimens.

The Roosevelts had a menagerie of pets in the White House. The First Family had a dog, cat, kangaroo rat named Archie, and calico pony named Algonquin.

Insect Observatory

Materials: box lid, crayons, markers, glue, construction paper or gift wrap, scissors, glue, hole punch, yarn or ribbon

Decorate the outside of a box lid with crayons or markers. Line the inside of the lid with construction paper or gift wrap. Copy, color, and cut out the insects. Glue the insects in the lid. Punch two holes along the top of your observatory. Lace and tie a length of yarn or ribbon for hanging.

A White House Menagerie

Materials: poster board, pencil, crayons, markers, White House (optional), scissors, glue, stapler

Unusual pets in the White House have included a lion. Copy and cut out a poster board shape booklet cover as shown above or design your own. Decorate the cover with crayons and markers. Or copy, color, cut out, and glue the White House on the cover. Cut same shape pages to fit in your book. Copy, color, cut out, and glue a pet on each booklet page. Write a story about each pet living in the White House. Describe how they lived, what they ate, and who took care of them. Staple the pages between the covers.

In 1903, Andrew Jackson, Jr., invented eye protectors for chickens.

The Wright Brothers made their first successful flight at Kitty Hawk, North Carolina, on December 17, 1903.

In 1910, Theodore Roosevelt was the first former President to ride in an airplane.

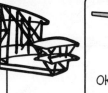

Oklahoma was admitted as the 46th state on November 16, 1907.

Insects

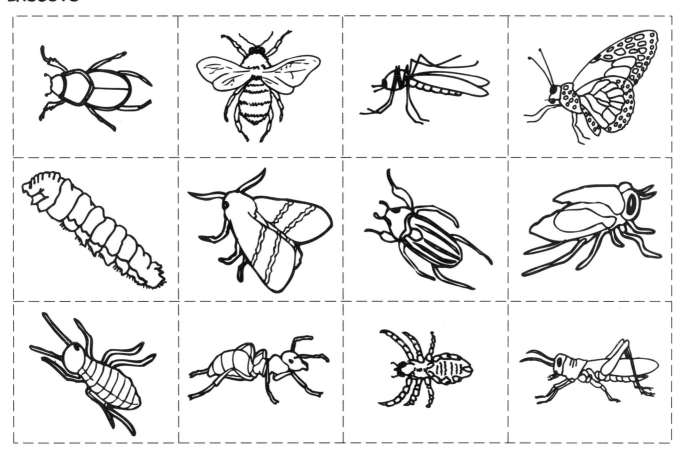

Pets

★★★★★★★★★★★★★★★★★★★★★★★★★★★★★★★★

27 • William Howard Taft
1909-1913

Born: September 15, 1857
Died: March 8, 1930

As a youngster, William was a baseball player. He was a good second baseman and a power hitter. President Taft introduced the custom of tossing out the first ball at the beginning of the professional season. Helen Herron Taft was responsible for the Japanese cherry trees along Washington's Tidal Basin. She personally planted the first two saplings with the wife of the Japanese ambassador, Viscountess Chinda.

A Cherry Blossom Forest

Materials: newspaper, red and white tempera paint, two small containers, sponges, scissors, poster board, green marker

Cover your work station with newspaper. Paint tree trunks across the bottom of a sheet of poster board. Cut a sponge into small shapes. Pour red and white paint into two separate containers. Dip sponges in either the white or red paint, or both. Sponge paint cherry blossoms on each tree. Use a green marker to draw a few leaves between the blossoms.

Our catcher, Marcia, put it right here!

Put It Right Here!

Materials: pencil, brown grocery bag, crayons, markers, scissors, glue, poster board, photograph

Copy or trace and cut out a grocery bag mitt. Color the stitches. Glue the mitt to a sheet of colored construction paper. Draw a picture or glue a photograph in the center of the mitt. Cut out a white poster board baseball. Attach it to the mitt with a tape hinge. Write a message at the top of your picture.

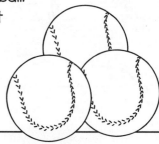

The Boy Scouts of America was established on February 8, 1910.

In 1909, Robert E. Peary reached the North Pole.

The American Presidents ©2000 Monday Morning Books, Inc.

Baseball Mitt Frame

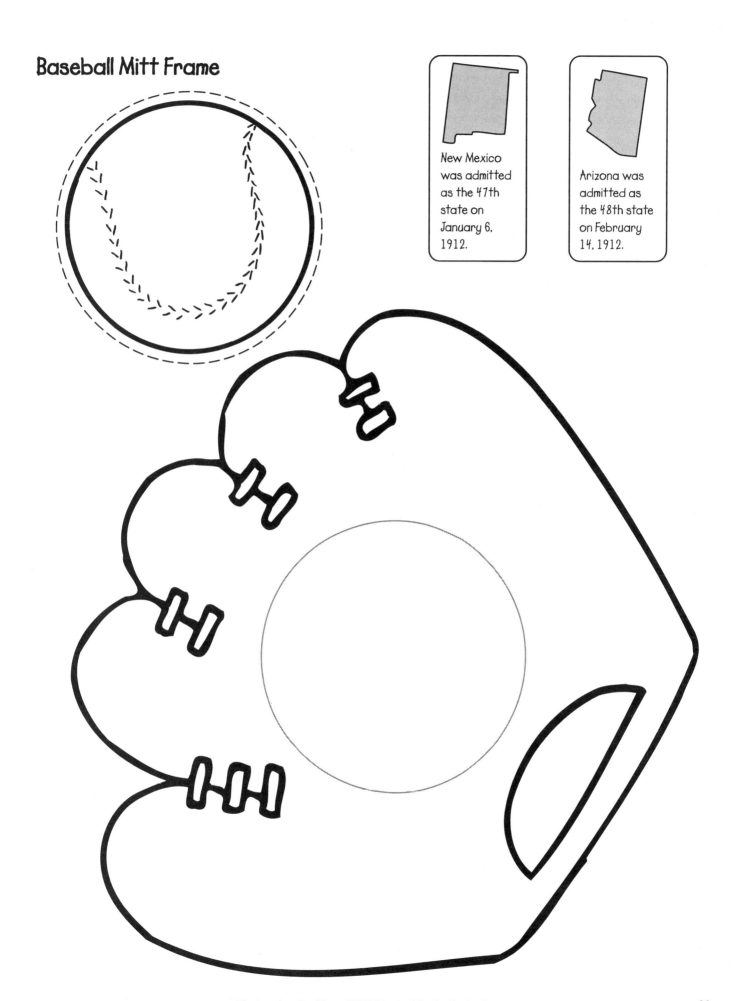

New Mexico was admitted as the 47th state on January 6, 1912.

Arizona was admitted as the 48th state on February 14, 1912.

★ ★

28 • Woodrow Wilson
1913-1921

Born: December 29, 1856
Died: February 3, 1924

President Wilson played golf for exercise. He also enjoyed riding his horse, Arizona. President Wilson's first wife, Ellen Axson Wilson, was a talented painter. Edith Bolling Galt Wilson, the President's second wife, observed the nation's wartime rationing efforts during World War I. She had sheep grazing on the White House lawn rather than mowing it. The wool from the sheep was auctioned for the Red Cross.

A Handmade Sketchbook

Materials: scissors, ruler, grocery bags, corrugated board, crayons, markers, glue, stickers, ribbon, colored chalk

Measure and cut several 5" x 7" grocery bag sheets to use as drawing paper. Measure and cut a 5" x 16" sheet of corrugated board and fold it in half as shown. Decorate the folder. Use colored chalk to draw pictures. Sign and date your work. Place your drawing paper and sketches inside the folder. Tie a colorful ribbon around the folder.

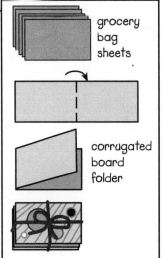

grocery bag sheets

corrugated board folder

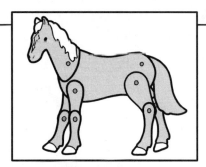

Animating "Arizona"

Materials: pencil, poster board, crayons, markers, hole punch, eight brass fasteners

Copy the horse puppet patterns onto poster board. Color and cut out the pieces. Punch holes where indicated in each pattern. Use two brass fasteners to assemble the body, head, and tail. Use one brass fastener to assemble each leg and a second to attach each set of legs to the body. You can change the position of the horse by moving the head, tail, and legs.

Sheep on the Lawn

Materials: pencil, poster board, crayons, markers, cotton balls, glue, scissors

Trace or copy the labels and doorknob hanger onto poster board. Make one doorknob hanger for each door in your home. Color and cut out the patterns. Glue cotton balls on each sheep. Write a message in each speech balloon to remind family members to save water and energy. Display your earth-friendly sheep in your home.

The American Presidents ©2000 Monday Morning Books, Inc.

Labels and Door Knob Hanger

Woodrow Wilson was the first President to cross the Atlantic while in office.

Horse Puppet

Body

Tail

Back legs

Front legs

Head

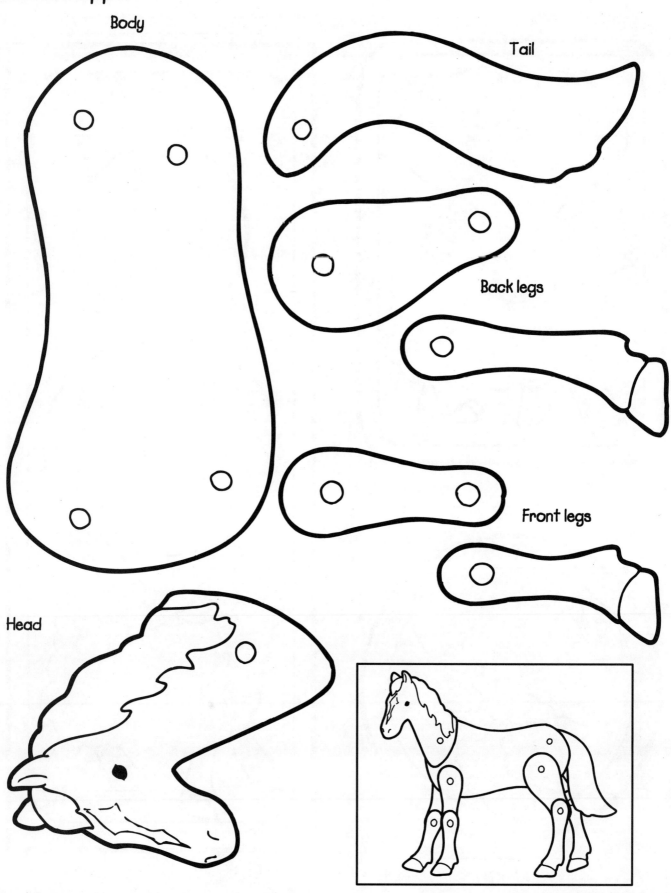

 The American Presidents ©2000 Monday Morning Books, Inc.

★ ★

29 • William Gamaliel Harding
1921-1923

Born: November 2, 1865
Died: August 2, 1923

As a child, William Gamaliel Harding enjoyed village life. His chores included milking cows, grooming horses, and painting barns. During his Presidency, Harding played golf twice a week. He also attended baseball games. William Harding was the publisher of the Marion, Ohio *Star*. Artists were experimenting with a new art style called Cubism. Natural objects were painted or drawn as simple geometric forms.

Our Family Gazette

Materials: paper, pen or pencil, photographs

Make your own family newsletter to send to friends and relatives. Here are a few suggestions for sections in your Family Gazette:

• Swap Shop-list items that you or your family are looking for as well as items you want to trade.
• The Chef's Corner-include favorite holiday, snack, and easy-meal recipes.
• The Learned Scholar-share school information, open house, special events, achievements.
• The Comedy Zone-create an ongoing comic strip, tell a joke, share a funny story.
• The Reading Room-write reviews about books you and your family have read, list books for trade or books you plan to read.

• Lights, Camera, Action-announce movies you want to invite friends and relatives to watch with you (include date, time of show). Write movie reviews.
• Inch Worm Report-Do you have a garden? Tell how your garden grows.
• Congratulations-list new members to the family, birthdays, anniversaries, graduations.
• In Every Issue:
  -Family network telephone numbers
  -Can you identify this person?-show a photograph, tell a story, or list a quote for readers to guess who it is.
  -The Poet's Corner

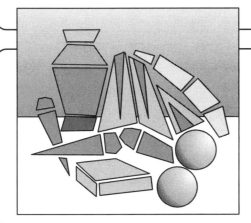

Cubing a Still Life

Materials: pencil, drawing paper, crayons, markers

Arrange a simple still life with three carrots, one banana, two oranges, a hand towel, a sponge, and a vase. Study the still life. Do you see a circle, a square, a rectangle, a triangle? Draw the shapes you see. Use crayons or markers to finish your work of art.

Newspaper Template

MASTHEAD

DAY • DATE   CITY • STATE   WEB ADDRESS

The American Presidents ©2000 Monday Morning Books, Inc.

Newspaper Template

SECTION • PAGE NUMBER

Newspaper Name   WEB ADDRESS   DAY • DATE

★ ★

30 • Calvin Coolidge
1923-1929

Born: July 4, 1872
Died: January 5, 1933

As a young boy, Calvin Coolidge earned extra money selling apples and popcorn balls. He like animals and often could be found in the White House with a kitten or raccoon around his neck. Grace Goodhue Coolidge was interested in education for the deaf and supported several children's welfare organizations. She also supported the Red Cross and Christmas Seals.

Shoulder Pets

Materials: felt, scissors, fabric markers

Copy the shoulder pets onto a piece of felt. Decide what color you want your pets to be. Do you want cool blue or a calico cat? Do you want a purple polka dot raccoon? Use fabric markers to color each pet. Name each pet and write its name on the back. Wear one pet on each shoulder or give one to a friend.

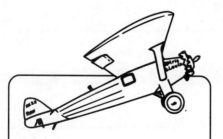

Charles Lindbergh made his historic solo transatlantic flight on May 20, 1927.

Popcorn Balls

Materials: six cups popped popcorn, sugar, water, white corn syrup, salt, vinegar, adult helper

First, make six cups of popped popcorn. Stir the following ingredients in a pot:

$2/3$ cup sugar
$1/2$ cup water
$1/8$ teaspoon salt
$1/3$ teaspoon vinegar
$2 1/2$ tablespoons white corn syrup
butter

Ask an adult to bring the mixture to a boil. Cover the pot and allow to cook for 3 minutes, until steam washes down the sides of the pot. Uncover and allow to cook until it is nearly to a hard-crack stage. (Drop a small amount of syrup into ice water. The syrup will separate into hard, brittle threads.) Do not stir. Remove the syrup from the stove and pour it over the popcorn. When the popcorn has cooled, press the popcorn into balls with lightly buttered fingers. Share the popcorn balls with a few friends.

The American Presidents ©2000 Monday Morning Books, Inc.

Shoulder Pets

Holiday Gifts Collage

Materials: paper, crayons, markers, scissors, glue, assorted gift wrap, ribbon, pipe cleaners, glitter, construction paper confetti

   Make a copy of the holiday seals below. Color the seals and cut them apart. Cut various shapes from gift wrap. Glue the gift wrap shapes to a sheet of poster board. Tie and glue ribbon bows to each shape. Glue a holiday seal on each package. Decorate the rest of the picture

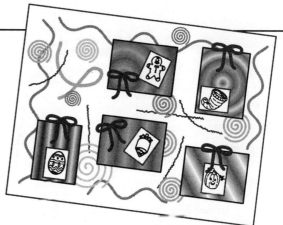

with pipe cleaners, ribbon, glitter, and construction paper confetti.

Holiday Seals

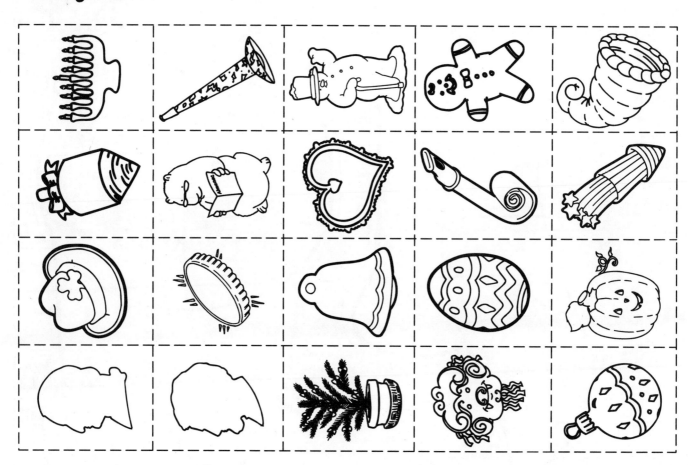

★ ★

31 • Herbert Clark Hoover
1929-1933

Born: August 10, 1874
Died: October 20, 1964

Herbert Clark Hoover had dreams of becoming a railroad engineer. He was also interested in geology and often studied a friend's stone collection. Herbert met his future wife, Lou Henry, at Stanford University. She was a geology student. Herbert Hoover enjoyed fishing and actively supported fisheries conservation. For exercise, President Hoover tossed a medicine ball.

A Rock Collector's Box

Materials: shoe box lid, ruler, paper, scissors, crayons, markers, glue, pencil, rocks

Collect and name rocks from places you visit. Decorate the outside of a shoe box lid with crayons or markers. Measure, cut, and glue a sheet of paper inside the lid. Draw a grid. Place one rock in each space. Write the name of each rock in each space. Make a copy of the rock collector's log. Write the name of each rock in your rock display. List the date and where you found the rock. For example: Savannah Sally—July 4, 2000—River Street, Savannah, Georgia.

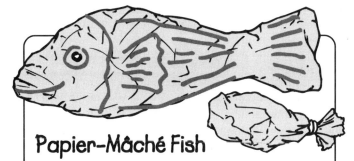

Papier-Mâché Fish

Materials: paper grocery bag, plastic grocery bags, newspaper, yarn, glue, tempera paint, markers

Cover your work area with newspaper. Loosely stuff a paper grocery bag with plastic grocery bags. Form the grocery bag into a fish shape. Tie a length of yarn around the open end of the bag to form a tail. Tear and glue newspaper strips to the fish shape. When the glue has dried, paint and decorate your fish.

"The Star Spangled Banner" became the official national anthem on March 3, 1931.

A Grocery Bag Medicine Ball

Materials: large white trash bag, plastic grocery bags, rubber band, permanent markers, clear packing tape

Use permanent markers to decorate a large white trash bag. Stuff the trash bag with plastic grocery bags. Wrap a rubber band around the open end. Fold, tuck, and tape the trash bag to form a ball. You will need a lot of plastic grocery bags. It may take some time to complete this project.

The first Moving Picture Academy Awards were given on May 16, 1929.

Amelia Earhart completed the first transatlantic solo flight by a woman on May 21, 1932.

Rock Collector's Log

My Rock Collection

Name _____ _____ Date _____ Location _____ _____ _____	Name _____ _____ Date _____ Location _____ _____ _____	Name _____ _____ Date _____ Location _____ _____ _____	Name _____ _____ Date _____ Location _____ _____ _____
Name _____ _____ Date _____ Location _____ _____ _____	Name _____ _____ Date _____ Location _____ _____ _____	Name _____ _____ Date _____ Location _____ _____ _____	Name _____ _____ Date _____ Location _____ _____ _____
Name _____ _____ Date _____ Location _____ _____ _____	Name _____ _____ Date _____ Location _____ _____ _____	Name _____ _____ Date _____ Location _____ _____ _____	Name _____ _____ Date _____ Location _____ _____ _____
Name _____ _____ Date _____ Location _____ _____ _____	Name _____ _____ Date _____ Location _____ _____ _____	Name _____ _____ Date _____ Location _____ _____ _____	Name _____ _____ Date _____ Location _____ _____ _____
Name _____ _____ Date _____ Location _____ _____ _____	Name _____ _____ Date _____ Location _____ _____ _____	Name _____ _____ Date _____ Location _____ _____ _____	Name _____ _____ Date _____ Location _____ _____ _____

The American Presidents ©2000 Monday Morning Books, Inc.

★ ★

32 • Franklin Delano Roosevelt

1933-1945

Born: January 30, 1882
Died: April 12, 1945

Franklin had his own pony at the age of four. He was a bird watcher and stamp collector. He maintained a collection that grew to 25,000 stamps in 40 albums. Occasionally he made suggestions for new stamps. Eleanor Roosevelt held her own press conferences and once served hot dogs to the king and queen of England. The Roosevelt coat of arms includes roses in a field which represent the family's name. And the motto reads, "He who plants must cultivate."

Stamp Collecting—One President's Hobby

Materials: pencil, paper, crayons, markers, glue, construction paper, loose leaf paper and notebook

Design stamps that relate to events or interests of the American Presidents. Copy or trace the stamp collector's page or design one of your own. Choose a topic and write the title in the banner. Color the banner. Draw, color, cut out, and glue your stamp designs on the page. Glue your stamp collection pages to loose-leaf paper. Put the finished pages in a loose-leaf notebook. You can also cut construction paper to fit in the notebook.

A Royal Picnic

Materials: 4" x 22" poster board, construction paper, buttons, scissors, crayons, markers, glue, stapler

Cut a 4" x 22" poster board crown as shown above. Wrap and staple the crown to fit your head. Glue construction paper jewels or buttons around the crown. Plan a picnic with family and friends. Bring along supplies for each person to make his or her own crown for a Royal Picnic.

Design Your Own Coat of Arms

a portion of the Roosevelt Family Coat of Arms

Materials: paper, crayons, markers, construction paper, scissors, glue

A coat of arms is a combination of designs on a shield. The shield may be divided into four parts. A variety of lines are used to divide a shield with more than one color. The colors used in a coat of arms are called tinctures.

To learn more about the history of a coat of arms, look under heraldry in an encyclopedia.

Your family may already have a coat of arms. If not, design one of your own. Copy the shield onto a sheet of poster board. Draw and color your design. Use color, images, and words that describe you and your family.

Lines used to separate fields of color.

Stamp Collector's Page

 The American Presidents ©2000 Monday Morning Books, Inc.

Heraldry Patterns

Shield may be divided as shown here.

Bend · Fesse · Pale · Bar · Chevron

Cross · Saltire · Paly · Bendlet · Party Per Pale

The New York World's Fair opened on April 30, 1939.

★ ★

Born: May 10, 1884
Died: December 26, 1972

33 • Harry S Truman
1945-1953

Harry S Truman really enjoyed reading as a child. His earliest memory was of chasing a frog around in the back yard. Harry took piano lessons when he was young. He grew to be a talented pianist. President Truman walked two miles each day for exercise. President Truman appreciated fine art. He especially enjoyed the work of the master painter Leonardo da Vinci. He did not care for modern art. President Truman helped organize the United Nations. Harry Truman's middle name was simply an S.

Chasing a Frog

Materials: green and white felt, raw rice or beans, black permanent marker, scissors, needle, thread, chalk

Assemble the frog bean bag as directed. Draw a hopscotch board on the sidewalk and invite a friend to chase the frog with you.

Wreath for Peace

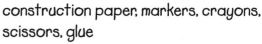

Materials: poster board, pencil, colored construction paper, markers, crayons, scissors, glue

Cut a large poster board circle. Draw a smaller circle in the center. Copy or trace the leaves onto colored construction paper. Cut out and glue the leaves around the poster board wreath. Copy or draw your own international flags to glue on the wreath. Write a message for peace in the center of the wreath.

A Frog's Tale

Materials: paper, pencil, light green and blue construction paper, scissors, glue, frog bean bag for inspiration

Write a tale about a frog on a construction paper lily pad as shown. Cut out and glue the lily pad to a sheet of blue construction paper. Let your bean bag frog rest on the lily pad.

The United Nations charter was signed in San Francisco on June 26, 1945.

In 1949, Reva Harris Keston invented a container to store used chewing gum.

The American Presidents ©2000 Monday Morning Books, Inc.

Frog Bean Bag Patterns

Trace and cut out the frog patterns from felt. Fold and stitch the body. Leave an opening to fill the bean bag. Assemble and glue the eyes, arms, and legs as shown. Draw eyes and a mouth with a black permanent marker. Fill the bean bag with raw rice or beans. Sew the opening closed.

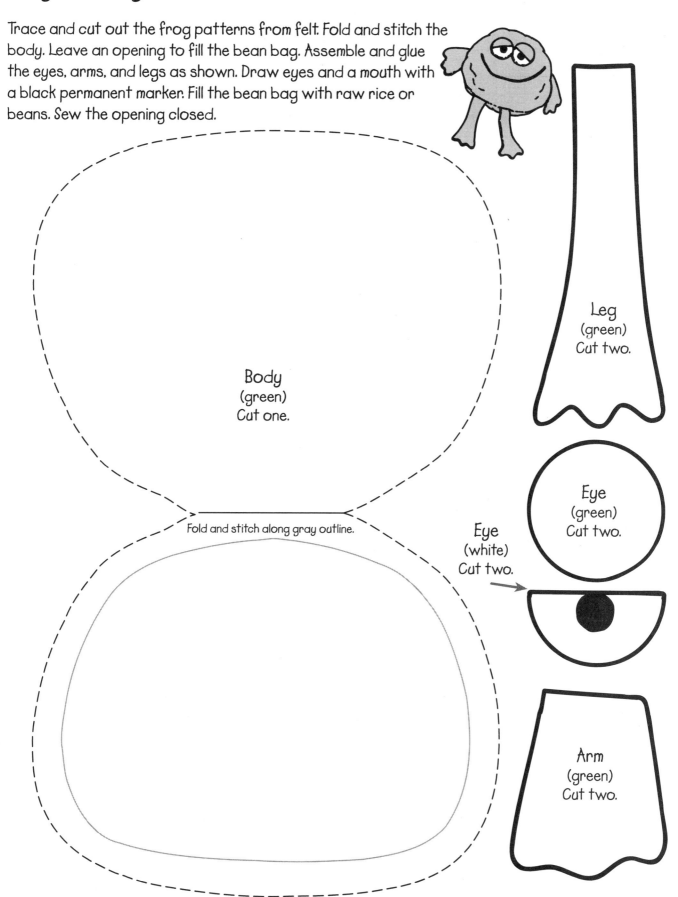

Body
(green)
Cut one.

Fold and stitch along gray outline.

Leg
(green)
Cut two.

Eye
(green)
Cut two.

Eye
(white)
Cut two.

Arm
(green)
Cut two.

Flags and Leaves

Ecuador

Norway

Poland

Venezuela

Mexico

Uruguay

Israel

Greece

France

In 1949, minimum wage was 75 cents per hour.

The inside of the Statue of Liberty is painted with lipstick-proof paint to prevent red lipstick graffiti.

Puerto Rico became a commonwealth of the United States on July 25, 1952.

The American Presidents ©2000 Monday Morning Books, Inc.

★ ★

34 • Dwight David Eisenhower
1953-1961

Born: October 14, 1890
Died: March 28, 1969

Dwight carried three lucky coins in his pocket: a silver dollar, a five-guinea gold piece, and a French franc. He wanted to become a railroad engineer. President Eisenhower's favorite pastime was fly fishing. He enjoyed sports and painting landscapes. A skilled chef, he was known for his vegetable soup and cornmeal pancakes. The First Lady, Marie "Mamie" Geneva Doud Eisenhower, brought back the Easter egg roll after a 12-year absence. Mamie Eisenhower used the color pink so much, it was called "Mamie pink."

Purple Mountains Majesty

Materials:
newspaper, old solid color pillowcase, 8" x 10" corrugated board, glue, wide brush, purple, white, black, and blue fabric paint, brushes, frame to fit 8" x 10" picture

Cover your work station with newspaper. Measure and cut an 8" x 10" sheet of corrugated board. Measure and cut a 12" x 14" sheet from an old solid color pillowcase. Brush glue on one side of the corrugated board. Place the pillowcase cutout on the board. Smooth out all wrinkles. Make sure the edges are secure. Allow to dry completely. Fold over and glue the excess cloth to the back of the board. Allow to dry. Choose a landscape to paint or draw. Frame your finished painting.

NASA, National Aeronautics and Space Administration, was established on July 29, 1958.

What's Your Favorite Color?

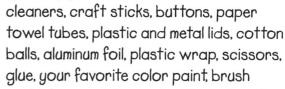

Materials: boxes, empty thread spools, pipe cleaners, craft sticks, buttons, paper towel tubes, plastic and metal lids, cotton balls, aluminum foil, plastic wrap, scissors, glue, your favorite color paint, brush

Make a sculpture using the materials listed above or any other materials you choose. Cut and glue materials, then paint your sculpture your favorite color.

Easy Vegetable Soup for Two

Materials: pot, large spoon, measuring cup, measuring spoons, 1 cup frozen mixed vegetables, 2 chicken or beef bouillon cubes, 2 cups water, 1 tablespoon fresh parsley, adult helper, 2 bowls

Ask an adult to help you measure and mix the ingredients listed above in a pot. Bring the soup to a boil. Turn down the heat and allow to cook until the bouillon cube dissolves.

The First Lady especially liked decorating the White House for each holiday.

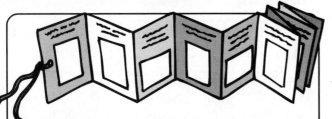

Holidays in the White House—An Accordion Book

Materials: 16 blank index cards, tape, hole punch, ribbon, pencil, paper, crayons, markers, scissors, glue

Assemble an accordion book as shown above. Hinge tape to the front and back. Punch a hole in the first index card. Lace and tie a length of ribbon through the hole. Make sure the ribbon is long enough to wrap and tie a bow around the closed book. Copy, color, and cut out the holiday symbols, or create symbols of your own. Glue one symbol to each page of your accordion book. Write a description, title, or short message under each symbol. Decorate the cover.

Alaska was admitted as the 49th state on January 3, 1959.

Hawaii was admitted as the 50th state on March 18, 1959.

Over 17 million immigrants passed through Ellis Island before it closed in 1954. In 1956, Bedloe's Island was renamed Liberty Island.

Dwight Eisenhower's nickname was "Ike." During the Presidential campaign, Mamie Eisenhower handed out campaign buttons that read, "I Like Ike." Another campaign slogan was "Ike Is Nifty."

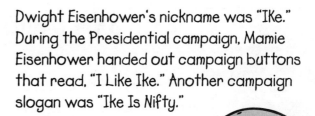

Design a Campaign Button

Materials: plastic chip can lid, markers, scissors, glue, tape, large safety pin

Copy or trace the circle below onto poster board. Design, color, and cut out, and glue your design to the inside of a chip can lid.

Create a Campaign Paperweight

Materials: plaster mix, glue, deep jar lid, poster board, scissors, paint markers

Mix and fill a deep jar lid with plaster. Allow it to dry. Cut and glue a poster board circle over the plaster. Decorate your campaign paperweight with paint markers.

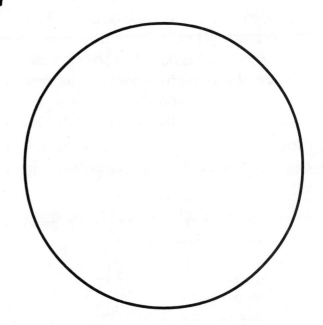

 The American Presidents ©2000 Monday Morning Books, Inc.

Holiday Symbols

★ ★

35 • John Fitzgerald Kennedy
1961-1963

Born: March 29, 1917
Died: November 22, 1963

John worked as a journalist for a short time. He read newspapers constantly and enjoyed sailing. President Kennedy was especially interested in the space program. The First Lady, Jacqueline Bouvier Kennedy, was interested in White House history. She started the historical restoration of the White House. In 1963, President Kennedy renamed and redesigned the Medal of Freedom. The new name was the Presidential Medal of Freedom. It is the highest civilian honor for contributing to the quality of American life.

If I Could Sail to the Moon

Materials: ruler, poster board circle, paper, pencil, scissors, construction paper, crayons, markers

Measure and cut out a 10" poster board circle. Use light colored markers to color the circle to resemble the moon. Copy or trace the sail ship onto poster board. Color, cut out, and glue the sail ship to the moon as shown. Glue the moon and sail ship to a large sheet of dark construction paper. Trim as shown. Write a story about sailing to the moon.

Quality of Life Medal

Materials: plastic coffee can lid, construction paper, star stickers, crayons, markers, scissors, glue

Design a medal to give to someone you think has made life better. Color, cut out, and glue a paper circle to fit inside a coffee can lid. Use crayons, markers, and star stickers to decorate your medal. Punch a hole at the top. Lace and tie a gold ribbon through the hole.

Sail Ship

In 1961, minimum wage was $1.00. Within two years, it was raised to $1.25 per hour.

The American Presidents ©2000 Monday Morning Books, Inc.

★ ★

Many people referred to the Kennedy administration as a magical time called "Camelot." America was enchanted with the Kennedy family.

Camelot in America

Materials: poster board, various size boxes, construction paper, scissors, glue, plastic straw

Collect a variety of different size boxes:

cereal box	cracker box
oatmeal box	checkbook box
bandage box	pudding mix box
cake mix box	gift boxes
tissue box	macaroni box

Cover the boxes with construction paper. Copy or trace the castle forms onto poster board. Color the castle forms with crayons or markers. Cut out, assemble, and glue the castle forms to the boxes. You may glue more than one castle form to each box. Color, cut out, and tape the flag to a plastic straw and attach to the castle.

Castle Form

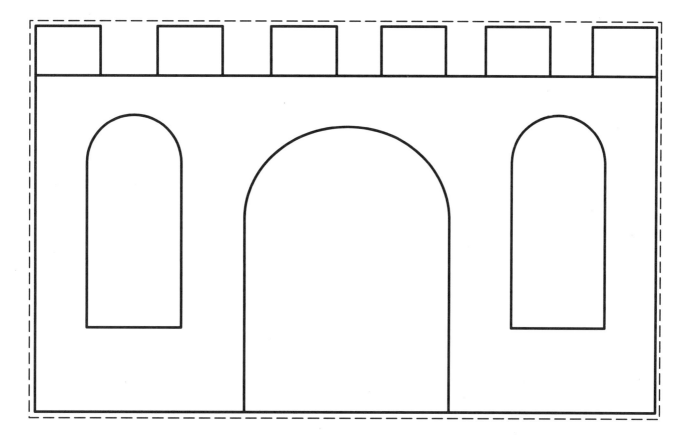

Castle Forms

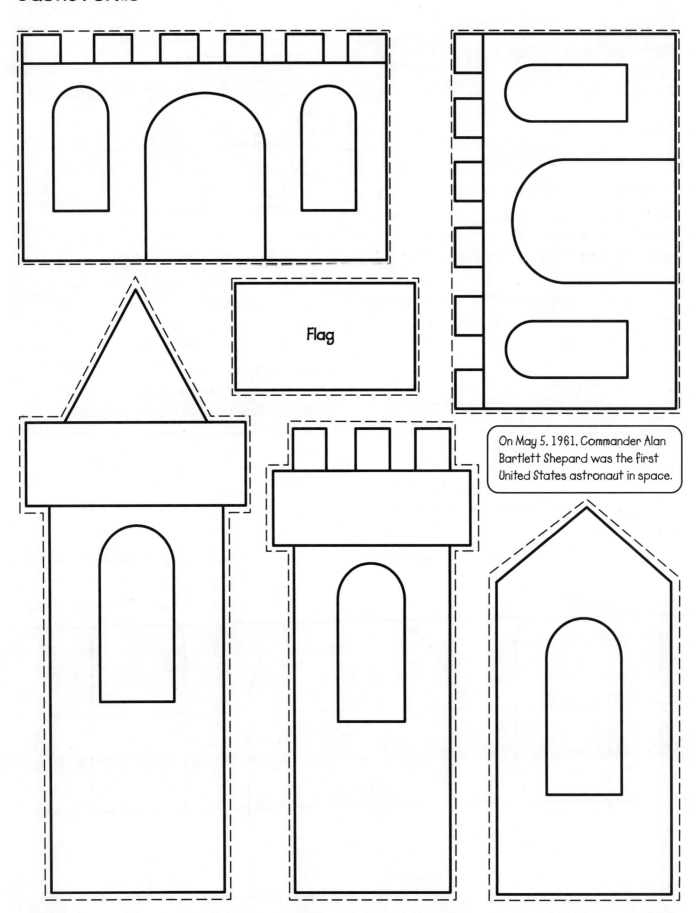

Flag

On May 5, 1961, Commander Alan Bartlett Shepard was the first United States astronaut in space.

The American Presidents ©2000 Monday Morning Books, Inc.

★ ★

36 • Lyndon Baines Johnson
1963-1969

Born: August 27, 1908
Died: January 22, 1973

Lyndon was a "crack marble shooter." He also enjoyed playing dominoes. President Johnson continued President Kennedy's plans to explore space, the new frontier. On June 3, 1965, Major Edward H. White was the first American to walk in space. The First Lady, Claudia Alta Taylor Johnson, also known as Lady Bird, was interested in improving highways. She encouraged planting trees and flowers along public roadways.

Texas Dominoes

Materials: empty cereal boxes, black marker, ruler, scissors, adult helper

Measure and cut 5" x 7" cards from empty cereal boxes. You will need 28 cards. Draw a line in the center of each card as shown. Set aside one card with no dots. Program the rest of the cards as listed.

- 6 cards with double dot sets as shown in the diagram
- 6 cards with no dots on the left and 1, 2, 3, 4, 5, and 6 dots on the right
- 5 cards with 6 dots on the left and 1, 2, 3, 4, and 5 dots on the right
- 4 cards with 5 dots on the left and 1, 2, 3, and 4 dots on the right
- 3 cards with 4 dots on the left and 1, 2, and 3 dots on the right
- 2 cards with 3 dots on the left and 1 and 2 dots on the right
- 1 card with 2 dots on the left and 1 dot on the right

To play, clear space on the floor. Shuffle the cards face down on the floor. Allow each player to draw five cards. Push the rest of the cards to the side of the playing field (these cards must remain face down). The player with the highest double set card begins the game. You must match the dot sets to the last card played. If you do not have a dot match, draw a card until you have one.

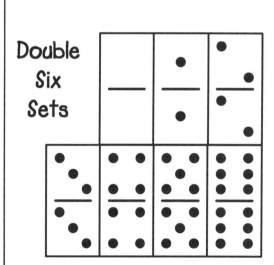

Double Six Sets

This diagram shows double dot patterns for a set of Double Six domino cards. Two to four players can play a game of Double Six dominoes.

The second New York World's Fair opened on April 22, 1964.

★ ★

On December 21, 1968, three American astronauts, Colonel Frank Borman, Captain James A. Lovell, and Major William A. Anders, traveled to the moon.

During Lyndon Johnson's presidency, the Clean Air, Water Quality, and Clean Water Restoration Acts were passed. All three were created to improve and protect the environment.

A Winter Holiday in Outer Space

Materials: aluminum pie tin, hole punch, yarn, star stickers, crayons, markers, scissors

Punch holes around the edge of a pie tin. Lace and tie four lengths of yarn to opposite sides of the pie tin. Gather and tie the loose ends in a knot. Copy, trace, or draw holiday symbol and outer space patterns onto poster board. Color and cut out the patterns. Punch a hole in each one. Tie various lengths of yarn to the patterns and attach them through the remaining holes around the pie tin.

A Breath of Fresh Air

Materials: poster board, crayons, markers

Design and decorate a poster to encourage others to be environmentally responsible. Use one of the slogans shown below or write one of your own. Use crayons, markers, and other craft supplies to complete your poster.

Environmental Awareness Slogans

One Earth—One Chance

Reduce Reuse Recycle!

Mother Nature Needs Your Help

Be Kind To Mother Nature

Water More Precious Than Gold

The American Presidents ©2000 Monday Morning Books, Inc.

Outer Space Patterns

★ ★

37 • Richard Milhous Nixon

1969–1974

Born: January 9, 1913
Died: April 22, 1994

At the age of 10, Richard Nixon told his mother, "I would like to become a lawyer." He enjoyed golf, bowling, and the seashore. On July 20, 1969, Neil A. Armstrong and Edwin E. Aldrin were the first men to land on the moon. In 1970, the Environmental Protection Agency was established to control water and air pollution. This agency also encouraged recycling. In 1972, President Nixon set out on "a journey for peace," to visit the People's Republic of China.

Soda Bottle Bowling

Materials: 10 clean and empty plastic soda bottles, paint markers, newspaper, masking tape, paper pad, pencil

Recycling can be fun. Collect 10 clean and empty plastic soda bottles to make a bowling game you can play indoors. Decorate the bottles with paint markers. Make a ball from crumpled newspaper, then wrap masking tape around the paper ball. Arrange the bottles as shown above and invite a friend or family member to play a game of soda bottle bowling. Keep score on a pad of paper.

Stars and Stripes on the Moon

Materials: round balloon, newspaper, glue, paint and brush, pencil, paper, scissors, plastic straw, round oatmeal box, crayons, markers

Inflate a balloon. Glue newspaper strips around the balloon to form a moon. When the glue is dry, paint the moon. Trace or copy, color, and cut out a poster board astronaut and flag. Draw a face on the astronaut. Glue the astronaut on the moon. Glue the flag to a plastic straw and glue it on the moon. Decorate an oatmeal box with crayons and markers for a base. Glue the moon on the base.

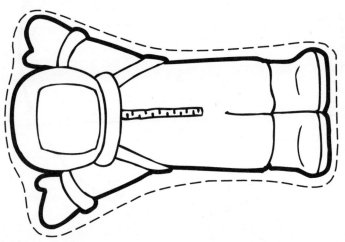

Finally there's a man on the moon!

The American Presidents ©2000 Monday Morning Books, Inc.

A Giant Gift from China

Materials: pencil, paper, crayons, markers, scissors, glue, construction paper, ribbon

Trace or copy and make two pandas.

Color, cut out, and glue the pandas to a sheet of construction paper. Color a 1" border around the edges of your picture. Glue a bow to the top of your picture.

Paper Quilt for Peace and Goodwill

Materials: 6" colored construction paper squares, pencil, paper, crayons, markers, scissors, glue, yarn

Copy or trace and cut out several quilt squares and doves. Color the quilt squares. Then glue a white paper dove in the center of each one. Glue the assembled quilt squares to construction paper squares. Punch holes along the edges and lace the squares together as shown above. Invite family and friends to help make a large Paper Quilt for Peace and Goodwill. Have them sign their work.

Quilt Square and Dove

President Nixon approved plans to develop the space shuttle on January 5, 1972.

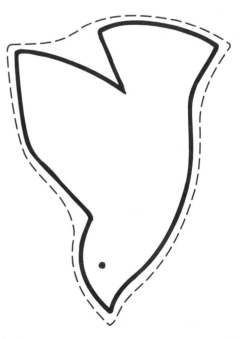

Panda

On October 2, 1973 America's fuel shortage reached crisis level.

On July 5, 1971, President Nixon confirmed the 26th amendment, which lowered the voting age from 21 to 18.

Richard Nixon was the first President to visit the People's Republic of China. He arrived in China on February 21, 1972. Following his visit, China traded two giant pandas called Ling-Ling and Hsing-Hsing for two musk oxen.

The American Presidents ©2000 Monday Morning Books, Inc.

★ ★

Born: July 14, 1913

38 • Gerald Rudolph Ford
1974-1977

Gerald Rudolph Ford was an athletic youngster. He enjoyed swimming, golfing, exercising daily, and skiing. In 1976, President Ford traveled to Independence Hall at Philadelphia, Pennsylvania, to review Operation Sail for the Bicentennial celebration. President Ford entertained Queen Elizabeth II of England and Prince Philip at the White House on July 7.

Bells Across America—A Bicentennial Mobile

Materials: shoe box lid, yarn, hole punch, crayons, markers, atlas, construction paper, scissors, glue

Decorate a shoe box lid with crayons, markers, and construction paper. Punch an odd number of holes around the edge of the lid. Lace and tie a length of yarn through the center hole on each side. Gather and tie the loose ends in a knot. Copy or trace the bell. Count the empty holes around the lid. Color and cut out the same number of poster board bells. Trace or draw, cut out, and glue a state outline shape on each bell. Punch a hole and tie a length of yarn to each bell. Vary the yarn lengths. Tie the loose ends to your mobile frame.

Garland of Bells

Materials: red, white, and blue poster board, construction paper, crayons, markers, atlas, hole punch, scissors, yarn

Cut out 50 red, white, and blue poster board bells. Punch a hole at the top of each bell. Trace or draw and cut out of construction paper each state to fit on the bells. Lace the bells on yellow yarn. Tie a knot in front and back of each bell to keep the bells from slipping.

Video games were first mass produced in 1975.

Gerald Ford was the first President to visit Japan while in office.

★ ★ ★ ★ ★ ★ ★ ★ ★ ★ ★ ★ ★ ★ ★ ★

Operation Sail was an international flotilla of sailing ships. On July 4, bells across the nation rang simultaneously for two minutes at 2:00 PM.

★ ★ ★ ★ ★ ★ ★ ★ ★ ★ ★ ★ ★ ★ ★ ★

And on July 7, President Ford danced a waltz with Queen Elizabeth II of England. The First Lady danced with Prince Philip.

Parade of Tall Ships

Materials: poster board, crayons, markers, scissors, glue, stapler

Cut a 2" x 22" poster board headband. Wrap and staple the headband to fit your head. Trace and cut out the tall ship patterns from construction paper. Decorate, color, and assemble the patterns as shown. Glue or staple the tall ship to your headband.

Shall We Dance?

The waltz is a dance inspired by music written by Johann Strauss and Franz Lanner in the 1800s. Dancers take one step for each beat and move in continuous circles around the dance floor. Study and practice the dance steps with a friend. Stage a performance for your family and friends. Invite them to join in.

Bell

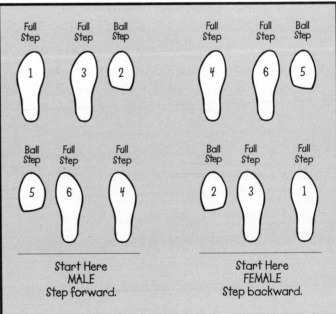

The American Presidents ©2000 Monday Morning Books, Inc.

Tall Ship

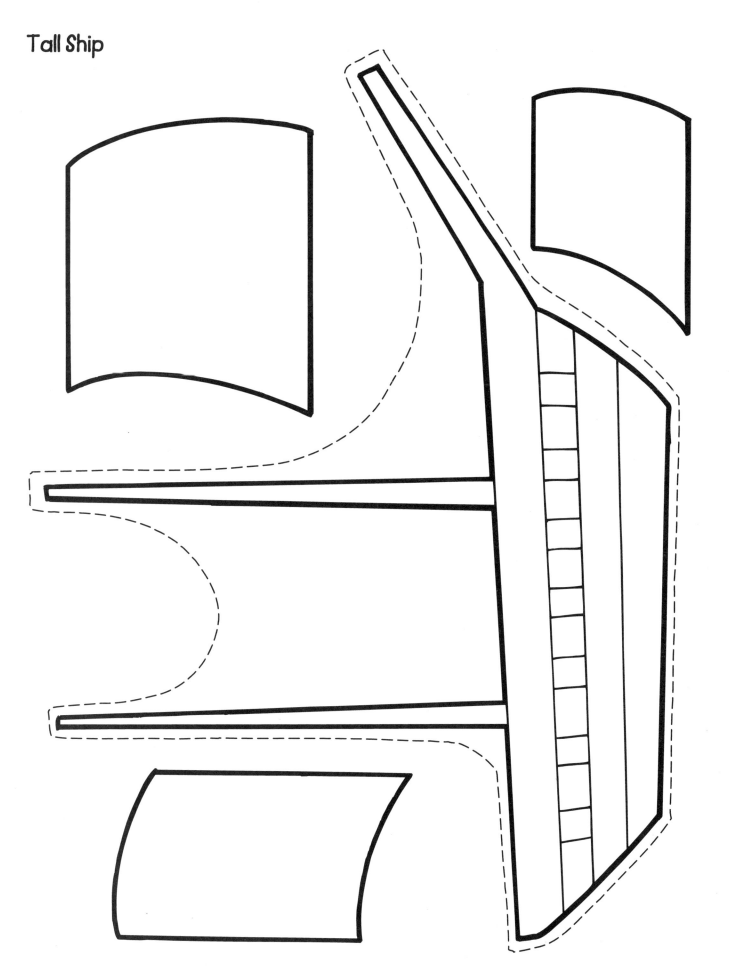

★ ★

39 • James Earl (Jimmy) Carter, Jr.
1977–1981

Born: October 1, 1924

At the age of five, James Earl Carter, Jr., sold boiled peanuts in Plains, Georgia. His nickname was "Hot," short for Hot Shot. President Carter enjoyed outdoor activities. He was also a speed reader. He often read three or four books per week. Rosalynn Smith Carter hosted picnics on the White House lawn. In 1979, she hosted a dinner to celebrate the signing of the Middle East Peace Treaty. In retirement, the Carters worked together in the Habitat for Humanity program.

A Peanut Picnic

Materials: poster board, paper, pencil, crayons, markers, scissors, glue, plastic straw, toothpicks, poster board, yarn, hole punch

Plan a peanutty picnic with your family and friends. Copy or trace the peanut patterns. Color and cut out each pattern.

To make a peanut medallion: Cut out a poster board circle and glue the peanut medallion in the center. Punch two holes at the top of the circle. Lace and tie a length of yarn through the holes to form a necklace.

To make peanut sandwich toppers: Tape a toothpick to the back of each peanut sandwich topper.

To make a flying peanut puppet: Fold the flying puppet along the fold lines. Apply glue to the tabs and assemble as shown. Insert a straw and blow the peanut up in the air.

To make a peanut headband: Cut a 2" x 22" poster board headband. Wrap and staple the headband to fit your head. Glue the headband peanut in place.

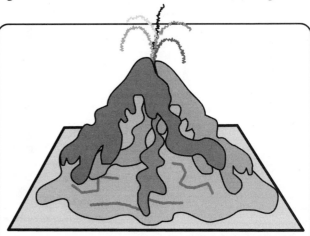

Mount St. Helens—A Rainbow Eruption

Materials: grocery bag, newspaper, glue, paint, brush, corrugated board, colored pipe cleaners

Cover your work area with newspaper. Stuff a grocery bag with crumpled newspaper and shape it into a volcano cone. Glue strips of torn newspaper to the volcano. Allow the glue to dry. Paint the volcano with rainbow colors. When the paint has dried, cut a small hole in the top and insert colorful curved pipe cleaners.

Mount St. Helens, Washington, began a series of eruptions on May 18, 1980.

The American Presidents ©2000 Monday Morning Books, Inc.

Peanut Picnic Patterns

Flying
Peanut
Puppet

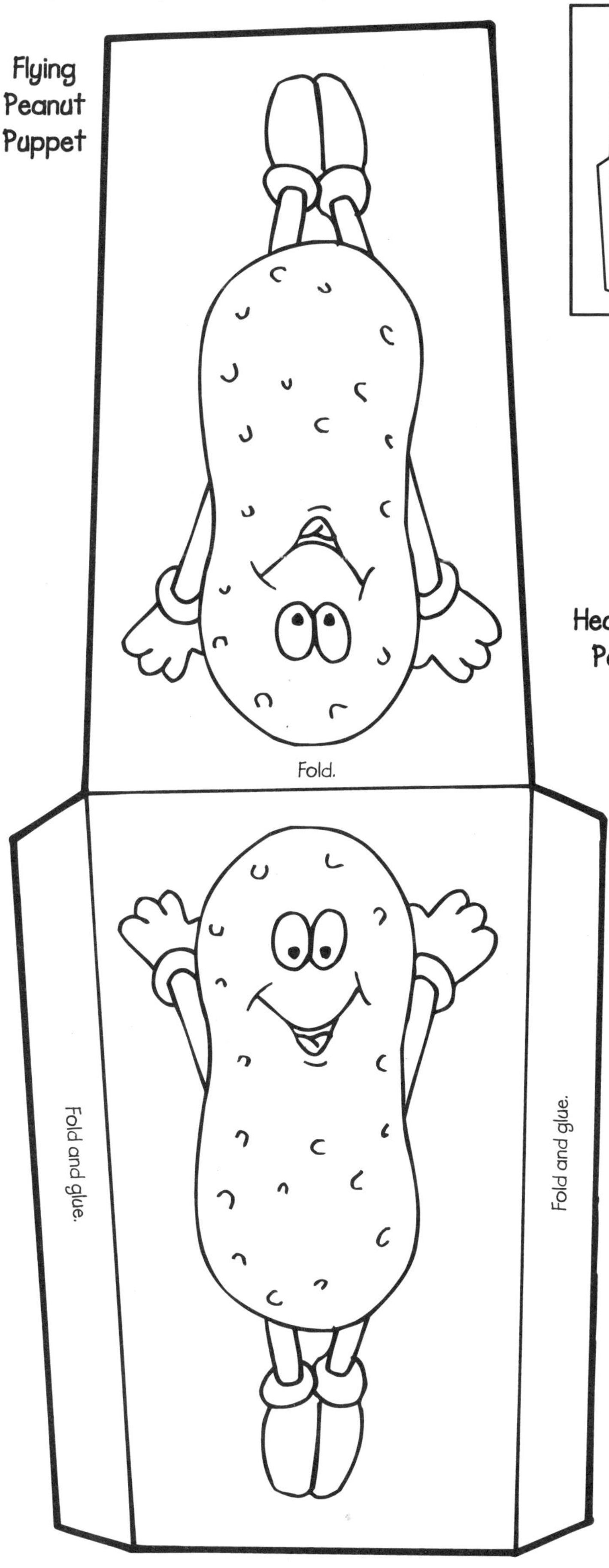

Fold.

Fold and glue.

Fold and glue.

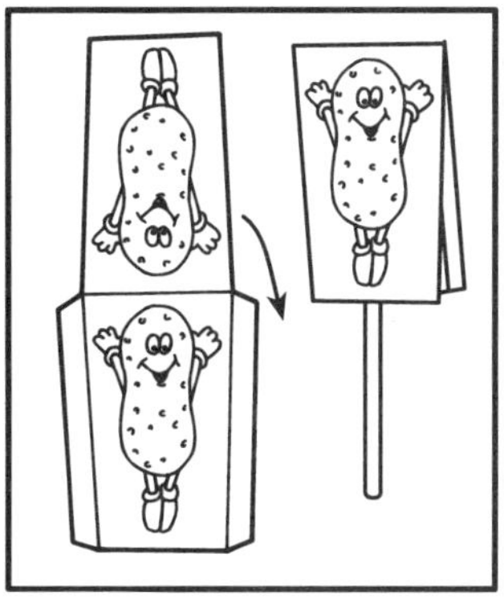

Sandwich
Topper

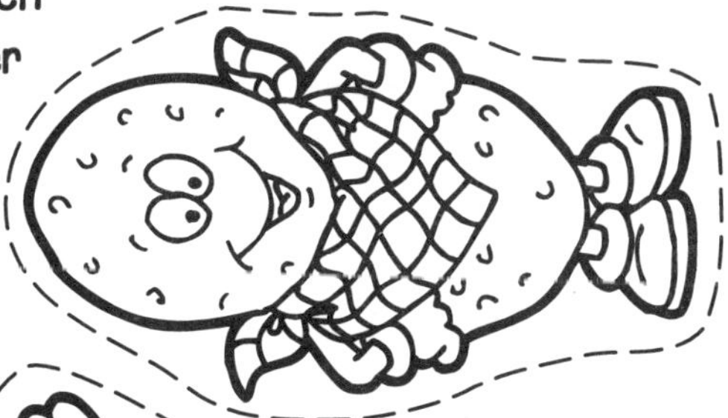

Headband
Peanut

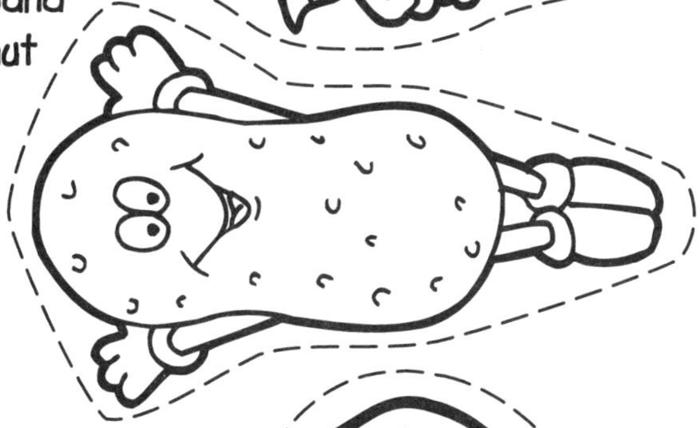

Medallion
Peanut

★ ★

40 • Ronald Wilson Reagan
1981-1989

Born: February 6, 1911

Ronald Wilson Reagan's nickname was "Dutch." Ronald enjoyed collecting bird eggs and butterflies and reading the comics. He also raised pigeons and rabbits and had a pet guinea pig. He once worked as a roustabout for the Ringling Brothers Circus. On April 12, 1981, the space shuttle *Columbia* was launched into space. In 1985, President Reagan and the First Lady entertained Prince Charles and Princess Diana of England. In 1983, the First Lady, Nancy Davis Reagan, started the "Just Say No" to drugs campaign. And in 1986, the President joined her on television to encourage a "Drug Free America."

Butterflies for "Dutch"

Materials: paper, pencil, craft tissue, aluminum foil, construction paper, scissors, crayons, markers, cotton balls, stickers, glitter, paint, brush, pipe cleaners, yarn or fishing line, tape, pushpins

Copy or trace the butterfly onto poster board. Decorate your butterfly with any of the materials listed above. Cut and glue pipe cleaner antennae to finish your butterfly. Use the following material combinations to create a swarm of beautiful butterflies to hang from your ceiling. Decorate both sides of each butterfly.

• Cotton balls and glitter–Paint a thin layer of glue on a butterfly form. Sprinkle glitter and attach cotton balls.

• Shimmering aluminum jewels–Color and cut out aluminum foil jewel shapes. Glue the shapes to a butterfly form.

• Torn craft tissue–Glue overlapping torn pieces of colored craft tissue to your butterfly.

To hang, tape a length of yarn or fishing line to the back of each butterfly. Use a pushpin to attach to the ceiling.

A Soda Bottle Shuttle

Materials: one liter or quart plastic soda bottle, poster board, crayons, markers, scissors, tape, yarn, adult helper, pushpin

Copy or trace the shuttle patterns onto poster board. Color and cut out the patterns. Fold tabs and tape the wings and tail to the bottle as shown. Apply glue to the back of the window and flag patterns and attach to the bottle. Ask an adult to help you punch two holes in the top of your soda bottle shuttle. Lace and tie a length of yarn through the holes. Hang the soda bottle space shuttle from your ceiling with a pushpin.

The American Presidents ©2000 Monday Morning Books, Inc.

Butterfly

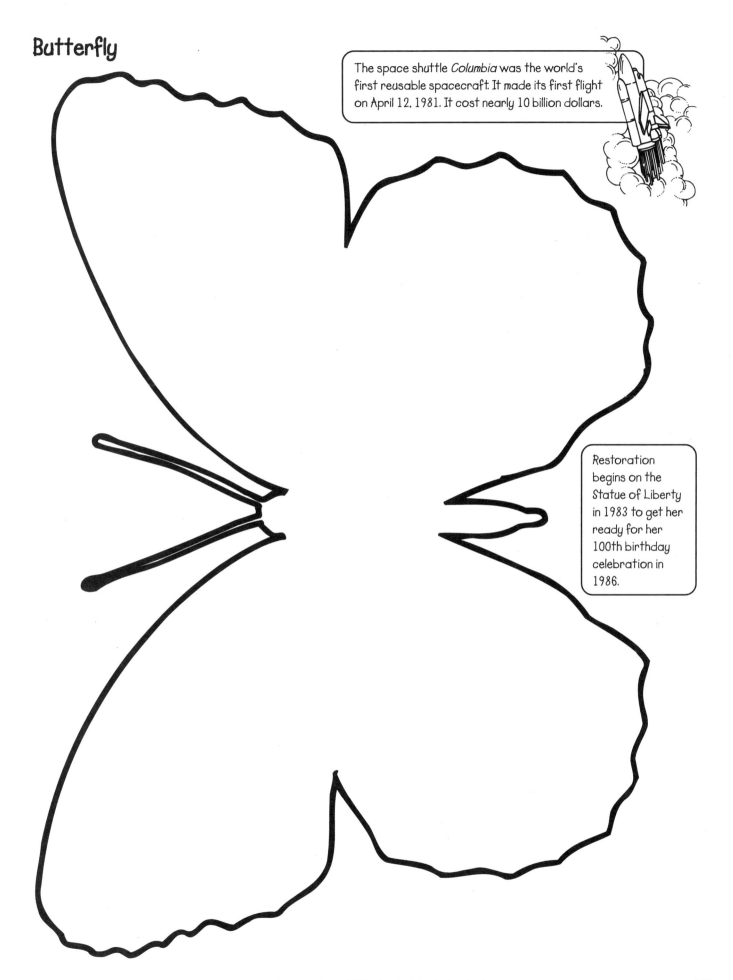

The space shuttle *Columbia* was the world's first reusable spacecraft. It made its first flight on April 12, 1981. It cost nearly 10 billion dollars.

Restoration begins on the *Statue of Liberty* in 1983 to get her ready for her 100th birthday celebration in 1986.

Shuttle Patterns

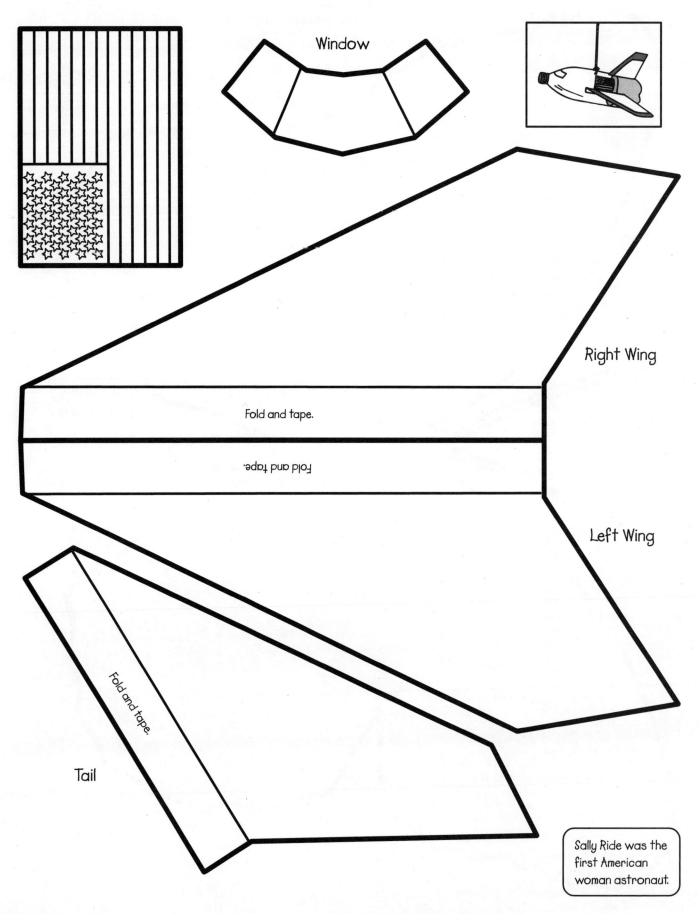

Window

Right Wing

Fold and tape.

Fold and tape.

Left Wing

Fold and tape.

Tail

Sally Ride was the first American woman astronaut.

The American Presidents ©2000 Monday Morning Books, Inc.

★ ★

41 • George Herbert Walker Bush
1989-1993

Born: June 12, 1924

As a child, George combed the beach looking for starfish. He enjoyed pitching horse shoes and reading works by C.S. Lewis. He disliked broccoli so much, one day he declared, "I'm not going to eat any more broccoli!" The United States celebrated the 200th Anniversary of the Presidency and the inaugural tradition. Barbara Pierce Bush worked to promote literacy for every citizen. She established the Barbara Bush Foundation for Family Literacy. She believed through reading and writing citizens can improve their own lives.

52 Great Books to Read

Rainbow of Books

Materials: 53 3" x 5" blank index cards, crayons, markers, scissors, hole punch, yarn, pencil or pen

Decorate an index card as shown above or create a design of your own. Punch a hole in the upper left corner of each card. Lace a length of yarn through the holes. Tie the loose ends in a knot. Read one book each week. Write the name and author of each book you read on a card. When all the cards are filled in, you will have a 52 Great Books to Read flip book. Share your flip book with a friend.

Celebrate the Presidency Fan

CELEBRATE THE PRESIDENCY

Materials: poster board, crayons, markers, glitter, construction paper confetti, scissors, glue, paint stirrer, stapler

Trace or copy the fan onto poster board. Decorate with crayons, markers, glitter, and construction paper confetti. Color and staple a paint stirrer to the back of the fan.

Starfish Pasta Collage

Materials: poster board, brush, glue, sand, pencil, construction paper, scissors, assorted macaroni

Paint a thin layer of glue on a sheet of poster board. Sprinkle sand on the board. When the glue has dried, brush off the excess sand. Copy or trace the starfish and shells onto construction paper. Cut out and glue the starfish and shells on the poster board. Decorate your picture with assorted macaroni.

The Soviet Union was dissolved on December 25, 1991.

Starfish and Shells

The American Presidents ©2000 Monday Morning Books, Inc.

Celebrate the Presidency Fan

★ ★

42 • William Jefferson (Bill) Clinton

1993-2001

Born: August 19, 1946

Bill Clinton enjoyed working crossword puzzles and singing along with the jukebox. One of Bill Clinton's favorite foods is peanut butter and banana sandwiches. President Clinton also enjoys reading and playing the saxophone. Maya Angelou read her poem "On the Pulse of the Morning" at the first Clinton inauguration. A pet cat named Socks lives in the White House with the Clinton family.

Make Your Own Crossword Puzzles

Materials: paper, pencil, scissors, glue, construction paper, adult helper

Make copies of the saxophone and cat graphs. Cut out and glue each on a sheet of construction paper. Ask an adult to help you write a list of questions and answers on a separate sheet of paper. Decide where and how the answers will fit and connect on the graph. Then program your crossword puzzle.

A Poem for a President

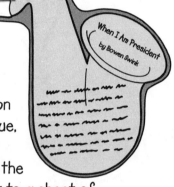

Materials: paper, pencil, construction paper, scissors, glue, crayons, markers

Trace or copy the saxophone. Glue it to a sheet of colored construction paper. Trim the edges as shown above. Compose a poem on a separate sheet of paper. When you finish, write the poem on the saxophone. Write the title in the mouth of the saxophone.

A Peanut Butter and Banana Party

Materials: bread, peanut butter, banana, crayons, markers, scissors, toothpicks, tape

Make a peanut butter and sliced banana sandwich. Cut the sandwich in quarters.

Copy, color, and cut out two sets of sandwich toppers. Tape a toothpick to the back of each topper. Stick one sandwich topper in each sandwich quarter.

The American Presidents ©2000 Monday Morning Books, Inc.

Crossword Graphs

William Jefferson Clinton was the first President to play the saxophone.

President Clinton's inaugural parade was the longest in history.

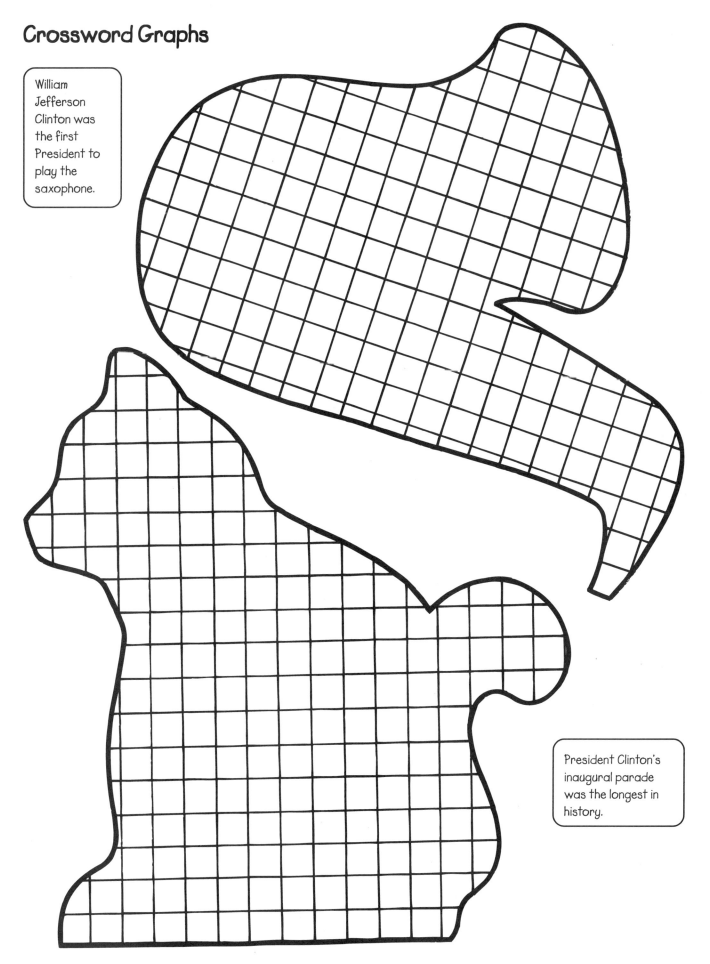

Saxophone

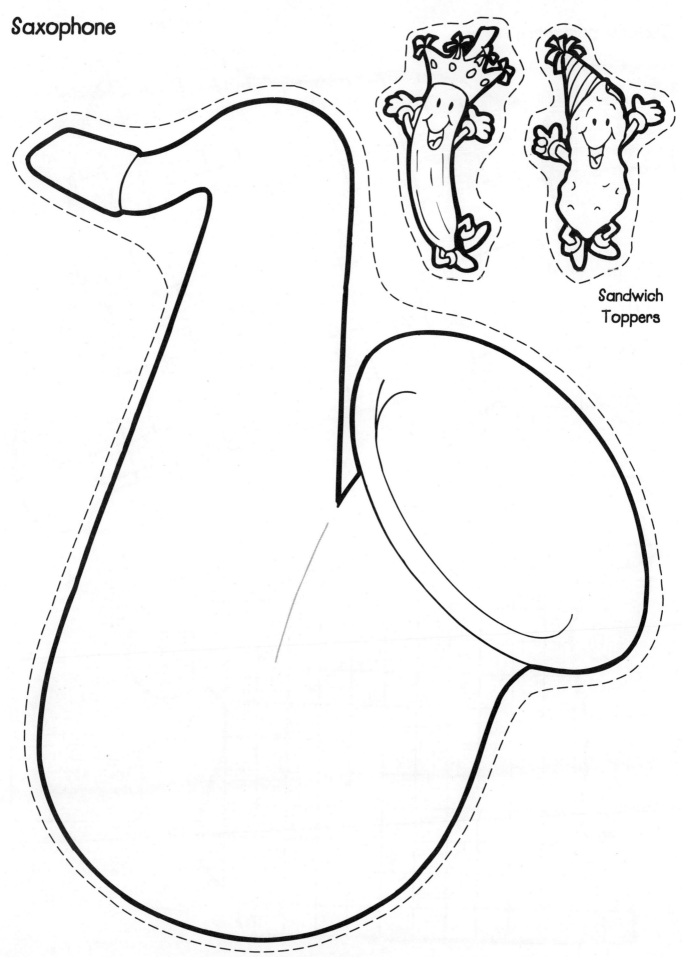

Sandwich
Toppers

 The American Presidents ©2000 Monday Morning Books, Inc.

President Cards

1-George Washington
1789-1797

2-John Adams
1797-1801

3-Thomas Jefferson
1801-1809

4-James Madison
1809-1817

5-James Monroe
1817-1825

6-John Quincy Adams
1825-1829

7-Andrew Jackson
1829-1837

8-Martin Van Buren
1837-1841

9-William Henry Harrison
1841

10-John Tyler
1841-1845

11-James Knox Polk
1845-1849

12-Zachary Taylor
1849-1850

13-Millard Fillmore
1850-1853

14-Franklin Pierce
1853-1857

15-James Buchanan
1857-1861

16-Abraham Lincoln
1861-1865

The Presidents' First Ladies

Martha Dandridge Custis Washington

Abigail Smith Adams

Martha "Patsy" Jefferson Randolph (daughter)

Dolley Payne Madison

Elizabeth Kortright Monroe

Louisa Johnson Adams

Emily Donelson (niece) & Sarah Jackson (daughter-in-law)

Angelica Singleton Van Buren (daughter-in-law)

Anna Symmes Harrison

Letitia Christian Tyler & Julia Gardiner Tyler

Sarah Childress Polk

Margaret Smith Taylor & Elizabeth Taylor Bliss (daughter)

Abigail Powers Fillmore

Jane Means Appleton Pierce

Harriet Lane (niece)

Mary Todd Lincoln

The American Presidents ©2000 Monday Morning Books, Inc.

President Cards

17-Andrew Johnson
1865-1869

18-Ulysses Simpson Grant
1869-1877

19-Rutherford
Birchard Hayes
1877-1881

20-James Abram Garfield
1881

21-Chester Alan Arthur
1881-1885

22-Grover Cleveland
1885-1889

23-Benjamin Harrison
1889-1893

24-Grover Cleveland
1893-1897

25-William McKinley
1897-1901

26-Theodore Roosevelt
1901-1909

27-William Howard Taft
1909-1913

28-Woodrow Wilson
1913-1921

29-William Gamaliel Harding
1921-1923

30-Calvin Coolidge
1923-1929

31-Herbert Clark Hoover
1929-1933

32-Franklin Delano Roosevelt
1933-1945

The Presidents' First Ladies

Eliza McCardle Johnson

Julia Dent Grant

Lucy Webb Hayes

Lucretia Rudolph Garfield

Mary Arthur McElroy
(sister)

Rose Elizabeth "Libby"
Cleveland (sister)

Caroline Scott Harrison

Frances Folsom Cleveland

Ida Saxton McKinley

Edith Kermit
Carow Roosevelt

Helen "Nellie" Herron Taft

Ellen Louise Axson Wilson &
Edith Bolling Galt Wilson

Florence Kling
De Wolfe Harding

Grace Anna Goodhue
Coolidge

Lou Henry Hoover

Anna Eleanor
Roosevelt Roosevelt

The American Presidents ©2000 Monday Morning Books, Inc.

President Cards

33-Harry S Truman
1945-1953

34-Dwight
David Eisenhower
1953-1961

35-John Fitzgerald
Kennedy
1961-1963

36-Lyndon Baines Johnson
1963-1969

37-Richard Milhous Nixon
1969-1974

38-Gerald Rudolph Ford
1974-1977

39-James Earl
(Jimmy) Carter, Jr.
1977-1981

40-Ronald Wilson Reagan
1981-1989

41-George Herbert
Walker Bush
1989-1993

42-William Jefferson
(Bill) Clinton
1993-2001

Monticello

Mount Vernon

Capitol Building

Lincoln Memorial

The Presidents' First Ladies

Elizabeth Virginia "Bess"
Wallace Truman

Mary "Mamie" Doud
Eisenhower

Jacqueline Lee Bouvier
Kennedy

Claudia "Lady Bird" Alta
Taylor Johnson

Thelma Catherine "Pat"
Ryan Nixon

Elizabeth Anne "Betty"
Bloomer Warren Ford

Rosalynn Smith Carter

"Nancy" Robbins Davis
Reagan

Barbara Pierce Bush

Hillary Diane
Rodham Clinton

Independence Hall

White House

Jefferson Memorial

Washington Monument

The American Presidents ©2000 Monday Morning Books, Inc.

White House

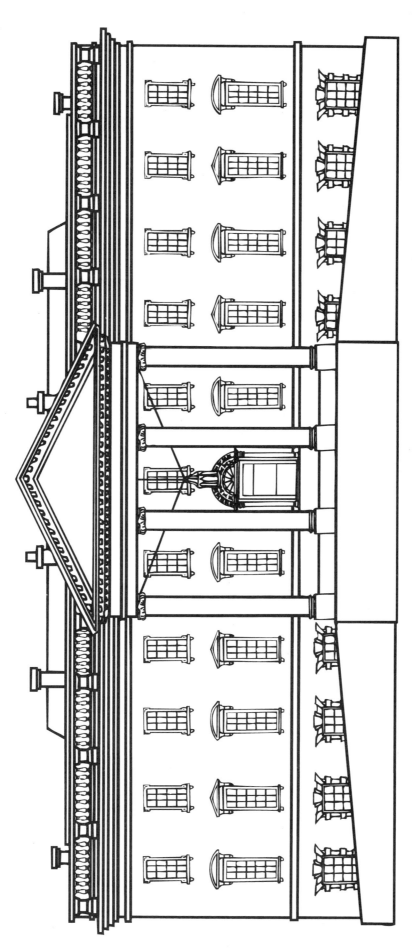

United States Flags

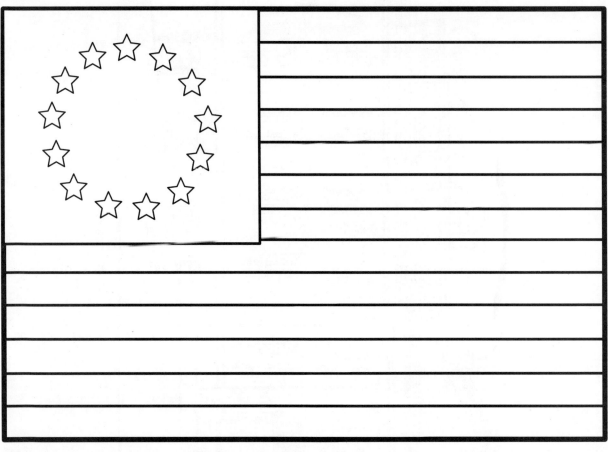

The American Presidents ©2000 Monday Morning Books, Inc.

The Great Seal of the United States

Presidential Seal

United States Map

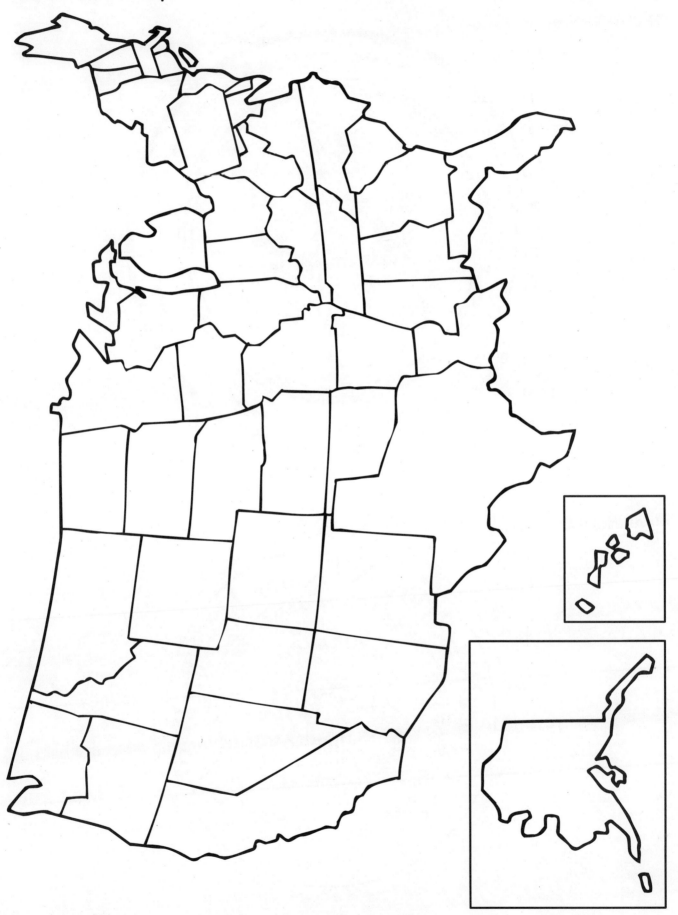

The American Presidents ©2000 Monday Morning Books, Inc.

★ ★

Bibliography

The American Presidents
   David C. Whitney
   The Reader's Digest Association, Inc., 1996

American Presidents: Life Portraits
   C-SPAN: www.americanpresidents.org

America's First Ladies
   Diana Dixon Healy
   Atheneum, 1988

The Complete Book of the U.S. Presidents
   William A. Degregorio
   Barricade Books, 1996

First Ladies of the White House
   Nancy Skarmeas
   Ideals Publications Inc., 1995

Illustrated History of the United States
   Sherry Marker
   Portland House, 1988

Our Country's Presidents
   Frank Freidel
   National Geographic Society, 1983

Presidential Fact Book
   Joseph Nathan Kane
   Random House, Inc., 1999

The Presidents of the United States
   Samuel Crompton
   Smithmark Publishers, Inc., 1992

The Presidents: Washington to Bush
   Greenwich House, 1989

The Timetables of History
   Bernard Grun
   Simon & Schuster

*The Young People's History of the
   United States*
   James Ciment, Ph.D.
   Barnes & Noble Books, 1998

★ ★

Chronology of thhe American Presidents

1-George Washington	1789-1797
2-John Adams	1797-1801
3-Thomas Jefferson	1801-1809
4-James Madison	1809-1817
5-James Monroe	1817-1825
6-John Quincy Adams	1825-1829
7-Andrew Jackson	1829-1837
8-Martin Van Buren	1837-1841
9-William Henry Harrison	1841
10-John Tyler	1841-1845
11-James Knox Polk	1845-1849
12-Zachary Taylor	1849-1850
13-Millard Fillmore	1850-1853
14-Franklin Pierce	1853-1857
15-James Buchanan	1857-1861
16-Abraham Lincoln	1861-1865
17-Andrew Johnson	1865-1869
18-Ulysses Simpson Grant	1869-1877
19-Rutherford Birchard Hayes	1877-1881
20-James Abram Garfield	1881
21-Chester Alan Arthur	1881-1885
22-Grover Cleveland	1885-1889
23-Benjamin Harrison	1889-1893
24-Grover Cleveland	1893-1897
25-William McKinley	1897-1901
26-Theodore Roosevelt	1901-1909
27-William Howard Taft	1909-1913
28-Woodrow Wilson	1913-1921
29-William Gamaliel Harding	1921-1923
30-Calvin Coolidge	1923-1929
31-Herbert Clark Hoover	1929-1933
32-Franklin Delano Roosevelt	1933-1945
33-Harry S Truman	1945-1953
34-Dwight David Eisenhower	1953-1961
35-John Fitzgerald Kennedy	1961-1963
36-Lyndon Baines Johnson	1963-1969
37-Richard Milhous Nixon	1969-1974
38-Gerald Rudolph Ford	1974-1977
39-James Earl (Jimmy) Carter, Jr.	1977-1981
40-Ronald Wilson Reagan	1981-1989
41-George Herbert Walker Bush	1989-1993
42-William Jefferson (Bill) Clinton	1993-2001

The American Presidents ©2000 Monday Morning Books, Inc.